Dear Nadi,

Wishing you own
'attractive' 2013

Love

Temsen

x

C000155747

THE ACT OF ATTRACTION IN BUSINESS

How to align your activity for extraordinary business results

TAMSEN GARRIE

The Act Of Attraction

First published in 2012 by

Ecademy Press

48 St Vincent Drive, St Albans, Herts, AL1 5SJ UK
info@ecademy-press.com
www.ecademy-press.com

Book layout by Neil Coe.

Printed and bound by TJ International Ltd, Padstow, Cornwall

Printed on acid-free paper from managed forests. This book is printed on demand to fulfill orders, so no copies will be remaindered or pulped.

ISBN 978-1-908746-49-8

The rights of Tamsen Garrie to be identified as the author of this work has been asserted in accordance with sections 77 and 78 of the Copyright Designs and Patents Act 1988.

A CIP catalogue record for this book is available from the British Library.

This book is available online and in all good bookstores.

What businesses are saying about 'The Act Of Attraction'

I've studied The Law of Attraction and I've studied for an MBA – both have missing elements. This book clearly and logically demonstrates how to combine practical business stuff with a deeper understanding of how our minds work to create a significant increase in performance. There's no fluffy stuff here. This is real, practical and usable material written in a detailed, yet highly accessible way. A landmark book has just been launched!

Tim Johnson, MBA
www.tim-johnson.co.uk

Tamsen uses her unique approach and talents to provide business people with a tool to create inspiring and unified business and personal goals. This is remarkable in itself, because these are traditionally difficult (and therefore avoided) necessities for anyone who wants to grow a successful business whilst enjoying the journey. This is a 'must read' for any business owner who wants to save time, energy, money and all too frequently, their sanity, en route to success.

Gill Bray, Business Hat
www.businesshat.co.uk

Reading this book was a real turning point in my business. Since reading the book, I have implemented the advice and in just three months, I have built a professional practice that provides both the income and the credibility I wanted. Most importantly, it has given me the tools to apply time and time again to achieve my future business goals. I recommend this book to anyone who has the desire to build their business regardless of where it is now.

Gary Johannes, Inspired to Change
www.inspiredtochange.biz

This book takes you on a journey and leads you through a process where you can create the business you truly want. If you approach it with an open mind and complete the activities, you will not be disappointed. I wish I'd had this book when I started my business 5 years ago!

Julie Owen, Jigsaw Business Services
www.jigsawbusinessservices.co.uk

The Act Of Attraction takes a pragmatic approach to an age old law – "what you think about you attract". Tamsen demonstrates the power of the mind and how easy it is to make your goals a reality. She teaches you how to take charge, how to clarify what you want and what you need to do to make it happen. It isn't enough to sit cross-legged on a Yoga pillow and think about your goals ... you actually have to get up and focus on exactly the right actions to get the results you want. Although this book is written for the business context it can be equally applied to any area of your life. This book teaches you the HOW which makes it very different to many of the WHAT books out there. It is a must read if you're willing to do the work.

Elvira Villarini
www.e-motionnlp.com

The Act Of Attraction is an essential read for anyone who wants to take charge of their own business success, rather than just going where life or business happens to take them. It is a practical book that guides you through a process instead of providing lots of airy fairy ideas.

Callie Willows, Digital Dogsbody
www.digitaldogsbody.com

Tamsen has been living, delivering and perfecting The Act Of Attraction, sharing it's principles with many, many businesses before ever putting fingers to keys to write this book. The result is a well tested, practical manual for getting results - with less stress, less wasted effort and more enjoyment. Having read and not finished some of the most well respected business books of all time I found the fundamental difference in The Act Of Attraction is that the process moulds around you, there's no rigid dogma to adhere to. The result for me? A stress free launch of a new venture, where I know exactly what I need to do and I'm motivated to do it, because I'm fully focussed on the result.

Ali Hollands
www.alihollandshypnotherapy.co.uk

Having always been one to reflect on 'what' I am doing, this book has revealed to me the importance of 'why' in the pursuit of success. This book talks to you, it reads your mind and senses your internal questioning, promptly coming up with the answer. Insightful, practical and quite remarkable.

Nick Hutt, HQ Mortgage and Finance
www.hqmf.co.uk

Since 'The Secret' much has been said of The Law of Attraction. This book provides a much needed reality check as it explains why in addition to focusing on our desires, we also need to take action to achieve them and it provides us with a set of tools to enable us to do so. Plus it's a damn good read!

Chris Hornby, Alpha Associates Ltd
www.alpha-associates.biz

ACKNOWLEDGEMENTS

I have so many acknowledgements to make, many of which do not relate directly to the book, but more to my personal and business journey that has enabled me to create and develop The Act Of Attraction itself.

So, firstly, I want to acknowledge every person I have worked with, whether as a colleague, a friend, a client, or a supplier and whether as a leader, a therapist, a coach or a mentor. Each one has contributed in some way to this piece of work.

I want to thank my friend and web designer Mike Morrison for inspiring me to write the book this year and for the initial cover design, which enabled me to create a vision that motivated me to take action.

I want to thank Mindy Gibbins-Klein, founder of The Book Midwife, MD of Ecademy Press and creator of the 'write your book in 90 days' process without which, I am certain I would not have achieved so much in so little time. Thanks also to Emma Herbert and Neil Coe for the book design and production.

I want to thank my family who allow me the space to be who I am and to follow my passion, and who provide me with my all important 'why'.

Thank you to my ten reviewers who committed the time to read my second draft in just one week and who provided the feedback which was crucial to finishing the book – the first ten printed copies are yours!

To my support team: a team created initially to build and lead a national business network, and which exists today as it did then: continuing to live the culture that we created together: open and transparent, collectively supporting and as inspiring as ever: Gary Johannes, Nick Hutt, Daryl and Paula Hine, Chris Hornby, Julie Owen, Lianne Dupre, Chas Jordan, Ali Hollands and Sara Otley. The continued existence and development of this unique team has been my rock – thank you.

And, lastly, to my friend and mentor, Tim Johnson, for being my greatest inspiration, for having unwavering faith in me and for consistent support and guidance – Tim, without you, I would be 50% as effective.

Contents

INTRODUCTION

My name is Tamsen, but my business friends and my clients call me 'Tam with A Plan'. It's a nickname I was given in my twenties and one that has followed me throughout my career and my life (no prizes for guessing why!).

The truth is, my planning began way before my twenties, and whilst it always resulted in the outcomes I **planned**, it did not always result in the outcomes I **wanted**. That's because in my naivety, I was misguided by goals which were based on what I **thought** would bring me success, rather than what I genuinely desired.

My personal journey has seen me pursue success to the detriment of my health and happiness, and it was managing to plan myself 'successfully' into being miserable that resulted in what has become a fascination with what specifically enables people to create outcomes that they truly desire.

Throughout my career, I have worked with hundreds of people in the capacity of a leader, a mentor, a therapist and a coach and each one of those people has taught me more about what enables success than anything I've read in personal development or business books.

What I have learned through my work (both with myself and with others) is that success in any area of life, including business, comes as a result of aligning 'internal activity' with 'external activity'. What I mean by that is that when you get what's going on in your head and what you're actually doing working together in tandem – that's when you get extraordinary results. And that's the basis of **The Act Of Attraction**.

THE ACT OF ATTRACTION

The word 'Act' refers to something that is being done or is to be done – it's about 'doing'. The word 'Attraction' describes what occurs when something is 'drawn' towards something else.

You may already have an understanding of 'Attraction' in the context of success creation as a result of knowing about the universal **Law of Attraction.** The Law of Attraction states that 'Like' attracts 'Like' and that you 'attract' into your life whatever you give your attention to. Whether that attention is through thoughts or feelings, or in some other energetic form, where you put your attention and focus is where you manifest results. Various books have been written on this subject and it was the best-selling book 'The Secret' that popularised The Law of Attraction in 2006.

This universal law is said to determine the order of the universe and our personal lives based on the principle 'like attracts like'. It states that when we experience thoughts and feelings, we send an equivalent energy frequency out into the universe and that the universe responds by sending back to us events and circumstances that are on that same frequency.

So, for example, if you have angry thoughts and subsequently feel angry, then an angry frequency is emitted and so events and circumstances that cause you to feel more anger are attracted. Conversely, if your thoughts are positive and your feelings are ones of happiness, you attract back positive, happy events and circumstances.

Now, if you buy-into the basic premise that we create our own reality, then this is easy to accept. We are all living The Law of Attraction, whether we are aware of it or not. Some of us are 'applying' it consciously and by definition therefore, with positive intent, and some of us are experiencing the 'effect' of it unconsciously.

However, The Law of Attraction goes further than just talking about how we perceive our reality. It also claims that desirable outcomes such as health and wealth are attracted into our lives through the way we think and feel, and that by simply changing the way we think and feel we can change our lives. That we simply need to be clear about what we want, visualise it and ask for it, believe that we deserve it and have faith that we will receive it, give thanks for it as if it has already happened, and it will miraculously manifest.

Whilst I have personally worked with The Law of Attraction for many years and whilst I have experienced successes which can be attributed in many ways to the way I think and feel, the most significant success I have experienced in my life, particularly in business, has come as a result of combining these energetic principles of The Law of Attraction with actual action, both in terms of what I say and what I do. So, whilst The Law of Attraction has many great principles, it alone is not enough to manifest success. Success is achieved when you combine the principles of The Law of Attraction with action (there is a reason why the word Attraction contains the word Action!).

So what is The Act Of Attraction?

The Act Of Attraction is a holistic approach to creating success. I use the word 'holistic' with caution since it is used a lot in complementary therapy and so, for some, it conjures up images of joss sticks and chanting! However, I choose to use the word because its real meaning describes perfectly what I actually mean.

The word 'holistic' is characterised by an understanding of the different elements of something as being intimately connected to each other and explicable only by reference to the whole. As you go through the book, you will begin to understand how each element of The Act Of Attraction is connected to the others and how without each other, their influence in the creation of success is significantly reduced.

It is worth defining here what I mean by success as the word 'success' means different things to different people. Success in the context of The Act Of Attraction simply means: "The achievement of something that is desired".

The Act Of Attraction is a based on the words embedded within the word ATTRACTION: ATTR**ACT** > **ACT**ION > TR**ACT**ION.

All three words contain the word 'Act' and the word 'Act' also sits at the centre of the word 'Attraction', so it's pretty fundamental to the process.

Whether it's what's going on in your head in terms of thoughts, what's happening in your body in terms of feelings, or what's happening externally in terms of behaviour, it's all 'doing'. Now, be clear, I'm not talking about performing here, or about putting on an 'act' – what I am talking about is the act of applying oneself **consciously** (both internally and externally) to create an outcome you want.

When you are able to get what is going on in your head and what you're actually doing aligned with what you truly desire, you can't help but achieve it. And this is where The Act Of Attraction is so powerful: It focuses your attention on the different elements that make up your internal and external **act**ivity and leads you through a process to enable you to align the two so that you begin to move forward with ease. The 'Attraction' bit comes about because in doing so, you create a pathway that both **leads** you to the things you want and also **draws** the things you want to you.

ATTR**ACT** is your **internal activity**. It is about what you want, what you believe, what you think and what you feel. ATTRACT is important because it's what drives your motivation and is therefore the basis from which everything else stems: because it's your internal landscape that drives your external landscape. Your thoughts are your beliefs in action, your feelings are dictated by your thoughts and all of these things drive your behaviour. What you believe, think and feel impacts hugely on what you attract into your life.

ACTION is your **external activity**. It's about your behaviour – the actions you take that other people notice and the perception that creates. It's what you say and how you say it, what you do, how you react and who you hang out with. ACTION is also about the intentional steps you take towards a specific goal.

TR**ACT**ION is the cumulative effect of ATTR**ACT** and **ACT**ION. It's what happens when your desires, beliefs, thoughts and feelings are aligned with what you are actually doing.

Traction is one of those words that many people use in business, but few can actually define. Some definitions of Traction are: 'adhesive friction', or 'the condition of being drawn'. Of course, it's referring to a vehicle or a load, but the essence is the same when the term is applied in business. Traction is adhesion (or 'grip') and **unforced** forward movement, and the reason it's so hard to define in business is because Traction often manifests as a 'feeling' or a 'sensation' before it manifests as a tangible outcome. It's that feeling we get when what we have been focusing our efforts on (both internally and externally) starts to 'grip' and we begin to feel like we are progressing forwards effortlessly. All of our actions start to impact in all areas and we begin to experience a gentle 'draw' as opposed to the forced 'push' that is so often associated with effort.

Another way to describe Traction is a feeling of 'flow' and I find that people are often able to identify with this more easily. 'Flow' is the mental and operating state in which one is fully immersed with full involvement and energised focus. 'Flow' is the ultimate in harnessing internal activity, because when we are in flow, our beliefs, thoughts and feelings are positively energised and channelled so that they are aligned with our vision and the goals and activities at hand. Other ways of describing flow are: *in the zone, on a roll, in the groove, on fire and in tune.* More simply: the opposite of being in 'flow' is being stuck.

Traction not only tells us that we are on track but it also gives us the faith to continue, and it provides essential momentum and focus so that we **remain** on track. It's like a snowball effect.

The best way to illustrate the power of aligning ATTRACT and ACTION together, is to consider what happens when you have one without the other:

ATTRACT without ACTION is like having a destination in mind but no fuel. Result = Stuck.

ACTION without ATTRACT is like having fuel but no destination or road map. Result = aimless driving or worse, wheel spinning!

TRACTION is ATTRACT and ACTION combined. It provides both the destination and the road map: it gets you in gear and sets the wheels in motion, it grips the road and it accelerates you forward.

I mentioned earlier that 'Attraction' is already working for you whether you are aware of it or not. You are attracting into your life people and circumstances, through your own activity, be it your internal activity: your desires, beliefs thoughts and feelings, or your external activity: your language, behaviour and actions.

Learning, and more importantly, applying The Act Of Attraction will enable you to deliberately attract to you and your business the things you want, by being clear about what that is and why and by having conscious awareness of what you are thinking, feeling and doing.

The Act Of Attraction is a process. And using the car analogy again, you might think of it like a journey. It begins with ATTRACT (internal activity) and is followed by ACTION (external activity) before culminating in TRACTION (the combined energy of aligned internal and external activity), and just like the state of Traction itself, the process of getting there creates the essential 'draw' conditions, propelling you forward to the next step.

Traction is more than desirable. Traction is essential, because you only really get moving towards your vision when your internal activity (intent, thoughts and feelings) and your external activity (actions) are in harmony, working together. And the best bit is that once you have traction, the effort required to keep moving is reduced... you gradually build up momentum, and once that momentum is sustained, it becomes almost impossible to stop.

It's a lot easier to move when you are already moving...

The Act Of Attraction is in two MAIN parts:

PART 1: ATTRACT and PART 2: ACTION and it concludes with TRACTION

PART 1: **ATTRACT**
(Internal Activity – what's going on in your head)

Section 1: YOUR VISION
Section 2: YOUR MIND-SET

ACTivities: The ACT Of ATTRACT

PART 2: **ACTION**
(External activity – what you're actually doing)

Section 1: YOUR BEHAVIOUR
Section 2: YOUR PLAN

ACTivities: The ACT Of ACTION

As I have explained, everything we think, feel, say or do is attractive. Whether it's attracting what we want or not is another matter.

When I use the word *attractive* (in *italics*) in this book, what I mean specifically is: *attractive* in the context of The Act Of Attraction and therefore, by definition, that it attracts the things that we want. I mean *attraction* that is both intentional and purposeful.

Be aware that this book may present some things to you in a way that is new, or different. You may find your inner sceptic makes an appearance or that you experience some internal resistance to some of the concepts.

Remember, The Act Of Attraction is about 'doing' and so the real value is in 'doing the work'. Whilst reading the book is an action in itself and will inevitably result in new ways of thinking, it is unlikely to be enough on its own to create a significant change in your life or business. The real value in is in the ACT element of ATTR**ACT** and **ACT**ION, which is why there are ACTivities for you to do at the end of **PART 1** and **PART 2**.

Of course, it is up to you whether you do the ACTivities. And if you do choose to do them, it is up to you how and when you do them. You may choose to read the book through first and then go back and do the ACTivities, or you may choose to do them as you read the book. It is not important which **method** you choose to do the ACTivities, but it is important (if you do choose to do them) that you do them in **order**. Equally, it is important that you commit your answers to paper. It is very common to think that getting clear in our minds is enough to effect change. It isn't. You can write directly in the book, or you can visit www.theactofattraction.com and download the relevant worksheets for free, it's up to you.

Through doing the ACTivities, you may find yourself thinking differently about yourself and your business (or your life). This is perfectly normal (and intentional), and whilst it may feel uncomfortable, those reactions simply serve to enable you to take what you have learned and to apply it in your life and business in a way that IS comfortable for YOU.

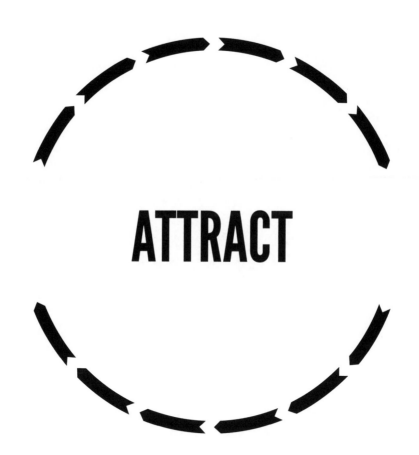

ATTRACT

ATTR**ACT** is your **internal activity**. It is about what you want, what you believe, what you think and what you feel. It is essentially your inspiration and your motivation and so it's the basis from which everything else stems. Your thoughts are your beliefs in action and both manifest in your feelings and drive your behaviour. What you believe, think and feel significantly influences what you attract into your life.

So, as it all starts in your head, let's start by understanding a little more about the human mind.

There are two components to the human mind: the conscious and the subconscious.

The conscious mind is the logical part of our mind. It is the part that we use to think, rationalise, analyse and plan and it stores our short-term memory. It is conditional, in that it will only accept a piece of information if it considers it to be acceptable to it and it is the part of our mind that we use to make decisions.

The subconscious mind comprises the rest. It's the base of our beliefs, values and feelings and it is the part of our mind responsible for all our bodily functions and systems. It is the source of our long-term memory and it retains details of all our experiences in perfect detail: that is everything we have ever seen, felt, smelt, tasted, touched or done. Many people find this hard to believe. I've been asked: "If my mind has retained the details of everything I've ever experienced, how come my memory is so poor?" Recall and memory are two different things. Our ability to consciously recall the details of every experience is not perfect. Our memory is.

The subconscious mind is unconditional, which means that the subconscious mind will accept a piece of information without any analysis or judgement and form beliefs based on it. So, whether an experience is positive or negative, destructive or beneficial, the subconscious mind absorbs the information without prejudice. It is incapable of analysis or consideration and therefore incapable of deciding what to accept and what to reject. It simply stores it as 'truth', on which it then bases belief. As such, when faced with a situation, the subconscious mind does not 'decide' which thought or feeling to react with. It simply acts in accordance with its belief system, regardless of the impact on us, or the situation.

The subconscious mind cannot differentiate between what is real or imagined and so when we imagine something vividly in our mind, a neurological pathway is created in the mind in exactly that same way as if it's happening for real. This process is one we use all the time, with both negative and positive results.

For instance, when you worry about stuff, you literally imagine the outcome you don't want happening (often in full technicolour, surround sound!). What happens is, the mind believes it to be real and so it creates the appropriate feelings and generates the appropriate physiological response, so that you feel bad. Often, if we continually worry about the same thing, we create these feelings over and over again and our behaviour is then directed to that which is conducive to creating that exact outcome.

So for instance, your family visit for the weekend and they leave to make the four hour journey home late at night. It's winter, it's dark and it's pouring with rain. You wave them off, saying the words "Drive carefully", and as they turn the corner, your thoughts are 'I hope the roads are okay tonight'. You go back inside and mention to your partner how wet it is. An hour goes by and you begin to worry about the roads, two hours and you're imagining wind, hail and sleet, another hour and your mind has an image of their car in a ditch. They are just thoughts, but now you are feeling anxious and so you pick up the phone to call them. Your heart is beating as you wait for them to pick up. Your body is responding to the perceived reality – in a completely appropriate way. Only, it's not real.

The same process occurs when we imagine positive outcomes. When we daydream or fantasise about winning an award, or making a big sale, or being swept off our feet, we experience the feelings that we associate with that. Children are particularly good at this, as their ability to use their imagination has not yet been tarnished by the conscious mind's ability to rationalise.

To the subconscious mind our thoughts are realities and so, whatever the focus of the conscious mind, the subconscious will present to it the feeling, or emotion, or behavioural reaction it associates with that experience, based on what it has learned and believes to be 'true'.

If you have ever been aware of thinking, feeling, saying or doing something automatically that you know is not in your best interests, or that you would prefer not to have said or done, then you have witnessed this process at work. We can all credit our instilled belief systems as the primary source of this kind of behaviour, yet most of the time we are not consciously aware of the beliefs we hold that influence our lives in negative ways, and many of us have no real understanding of how we develop these beliefs that are so incredibly powerful.

From the minute we enter the world, we receive constant suggestions through our senses: sight, sound, smell, taste and touch. As we develop, we form belief systems based on these experiences and this is called autosuggestion. Our thoughts, feelings and behavioural responses are then determined by the belief systems we hold in our subconscious mind.

If, for example, a person is told continually as a child that they are just like their mother, they are likely to form a belief that this is the case. If that same person also witnessed arguments between their parents, where the mother was labelled 'controlling', then over time, they will likely form an association between their mother's negative personality traits and their own personality, believing that they are also controlling. Equally, if a person is told from early childhood that they are brave and capable, they are likely to grow up to believe it (as long as nothing occurs later to contradict it), and as behaviour is driven by belief, they will behave bravely and capably. This is the power of the mind.

The mind plays a crucial part in The Act Of Attraction and particularly in ATTRACT, which looks at the two elements of your internal activity: YOUR VISION and YOUR MIND-SET.

YOUR VISION

A vision is a mental image produced by the imagination and it's usually a long-term view of the future. In a business context, it's a picture of how the owner wants their business to be in the future.

Many people have a vision. However, not all visions are effective. When I talk about 'a vision' and 'visioning' in this book, I am talking about it in the context of The Act Of Attraction – I am talking about an *attractive* one.

An *attractive* vision conveys the *intent* of the business and because it is forward focused, it sets the direction. It includes the *purpose* of the business and, as a result, a framework within which decisions are made. It provides the basis of the strategy and all activity going forward, but, most importantly in the context of The Act Of Attraction, an *attractive* vision is one that **motivates the people in the business to take action.** If a vision doesn't motivate action, then it is not *attractive*.

I have been working with visioning for many years now and the power of it still excites me. It was visioning that resulted in my dramatic life-change back in 2002. It enabled me to grow my first small business in 2007 and it played a huge part in the extraordinary success of the National Business Network I was involved in leading and developing nationally, between 2007 and 2011.

So, why is visioning so powerful?

People with an *attractive* vision have a 'bigger picture' perspective on their business. They have a compass point in the future to move towards which means that they have more direction than those without.

This means that their focus is 'on' their business as well as 'in' it which means that they go beyond what they might think is possible, stepping out of their comfort zone, enabling them to make important decisions more easily. Because their vision includes their intent ('what') and their purpose ('why'), they are more likely to set goals and create a plan of action ('how') to achieve them. This results in activity that is intentional and purposeful and therefore more likely to produce the intended outcome.

Many of the business people I work with come to me because they are frustrated with the lack of success in their business. They describe their busy diary and their immense activity but they tell me that fundamentally they're not 'getting anywhere'. When asked the question: "Where specifically do you want to be 'getting'?" they often can't tell me. Therein lies the first problem.

Not having a vision for your business is like handing over responsibility for your business's success to other people and circumstances. When you design your business vision yourself, you take control of your business (and your life!).

Your vision is about knowing where you're heading and why, and designing your vision for the business and life you want is imperative if you are to create it.

How does visioning work?

You'll recall that the subconscious mind does not know the difference between what is real and what is imagined. When we imagine something vividly in our mind, a neurological pathway is created in exactly that same way as if it's happening for real.

We can use this process in a conscious way to attract outcomes that we actually want by imagining vividly, in full technicolour and surround sound, those things. When we imagine the outcome exactly as we want it to be, we create the images and feelings that go with that outcome. Our subconscious mind then responds with the relevant physiological reaction and directs our behaviour to that which is conducive to attracting the people and opportunities that make that outcome a reality.

This is visioning in the context of The Act Of Attraction. It is not enough to simply imagine the outcomes you want and to feel the way you would if it were real. A vision that is *attractive* is one that motivates you to also *behave* in a way that will attract to you the things that will make the vision a reality.

Designing your *attractive* Vision

As I said earlier, a vision is a picture of how the business looks in the future. A vision provides a compass point in the distance to move towards, but it does not provide the steps required to get there. It contains the 'what' and the 'why', but not the 'how'. Visioning is not about 'how' and, in fact, focusing on 'how' is likely to get in the way of creating a motivating vision. We'll cover 'how' when we get to PART 2: ACTION.

For some people visioning is easy. They are able to design a complete visual picture, in their mind, with specific details, including the environment, people, financial income, dates, timescales and awards won, etc. However, not everyone knows exactly where they want to be in their business and for those people visioning can be more challenging.

Admittedly, the clearer and more specific your vision, the more powerful and motivating it'll be. But, a vision does not have to be all singing, all dancing to be motivating. The truth is I didn't embark on my business journey with a completely defined and detailed vision. What I did have though was clarity of *intent* and a strong sense of *purpose* and, as a result, my goals were aligned with those things and so my activity generated the outcomes I intended.

I have worked with many business owners on their business vision and everyone is different. Some are incredibly detailed and others are more conceptual. Some are very business focused and others are focused more on the impact of the business's success on their life and family. There isn't a 'one size fits all' way to design a vision and yours will be different to anyone else's. As long as your vision **motivates you to take action,** it will do its job.

In order to ensure that your vision motivates you to take action, it needs to be based on two things: 1. Your *intent* ('what' you want) and 2. Your *purpose* ('why' you want it). When you have a vision based on both those things, it cannot fail to motivate you.

INTENT (your 'what')

Having *intent* is the same as having *goals*. Both words describe the 'what' – the outcome or achievement upon which effort is focused.

Your intent is a large part of your vision and so it must reflect outcomes that you strongly desire. I say 'desire', because 'desire' describes the things that we 'want' (including who we want to 'be' and how we want to 'feel'), rather than things that we 'need'. It is worth pointing out the difference: a 'need' is something that is *required* in order to survive, whereas a 'want' is something that is *desired* as opposed to *required*.

If you've ever been in sales, you'll know that 'want' is a far greater motivator than 'need', so whilst some aspects of your intent will inevitably be based on needs (I know you need to make a certain amount of revenue to pay the bills!), your vision will be more powerful if it also leverages the things you really want.

Many people rarely stop to ask themselves what they really want – instead, they let life happen to them. In my experience this is for one of two reasons: 1. They don't believe that they have the power to create their own happiness or success, and 2. They are focused on what they don't want instead of what they do want.

The irony is that they are all already attracting everything they have into their life, and often it's not what they would choose. I find that once people accept that they are already attracting, they begin to attract based on their desire – after all, what have they got to lose?

I mentioned earlier that 'wants' include who we want to be. This is important. Who we are, plays a huge part in what we achieve and therefore plays an important part in visioning. I also mentioned earlier that 'wants' include how we want to feel. Actually, the real truth is that our wants are ALL about feelings. Ultimately, we are 'feeling' beings – we do stuff in order to feel good and so when we come up with our goals, they are always driven by our innate desire to experience a certain feeling – always. I'll repeat that because it's important: Everything you do, have and say is with the intent of generating a desired feeling. This is why it is also important that your wants are your own and not the wants of others.

Sometimes people start a business only to find later on that their intent is based on the goals of their parents, or their partner, or on the expectations of others. One client said to me once "I need to see five clients a day every day." She said it three times during a one-hour coaching call. When questioned, she told me that her 'need' was based on the income she needed to earn in a week and so I asked her "Do you want to see five clients a day every day?" She admitted that seeing 25 clients a week was not what she wanted at all. When I drilled down further, it became clear that her husband had told her that seeing 25 clients per week was what she needed to do to make a success of her business. So, we had two issues: 1. Her drive was based on 'need' as opposed to 'want', and 2. The perceived 'want' was her husband's and not hers! After explaining that a vision based entirely on need was not as strong as a vision based also on want, I asked her how many clients she wanted to work with. She said that 12 clients a week over three working days was desirable. So, we started there and began to look at other ways for her to meet her income needs that also leveraged her own genuine 'wants'.

It's pointless building a vision around stuff that you do not genuinely want. You might do your best to achieve it, but you will not attract to your business the things you truly desire and you are unlikely therefore to be truly happy or satisfied.

Perhaps this resonates with you? Perhaps you are already doing things or aiming for outcomes based on the wants or expectations of others. We've all done it – I know I have. Perhaps now is the time to look at the things you are doing or aiming for and decide which you're going to keep and which you are going to discard?

Your path to genuine success is one that is authentic, and by that I mean one that is based on what you truly want for yourself, and not based on any ones else's measure of success (even if you are married to them!).

Discovering your intent

To discover your intent (or the intent of your business), it's important for you to focus on desire. What do you really **want** your business to be like? Later we will look at 'why' which is also important, but for now we are concerned with 'what'.

Remember, at this stage, we are not concerned with 'how' either. The reason for this is that whilst working out how we will achieve something is clearly an essential part of creating outcomes (and something we will cover in detail in this book), being concerned with it at this stage can get in the way of defining the 'what', especially for the more practical amongst us.

Many of the outcomes I've attracted have occurred when I have only known 'what' I wanted with no idea of how I would make it happen.

"I want to live in a house near a city by the sea."

I remember making the decision to leave Melbourne after four years of living, studying and working there. Returning to the UK after four years away was a scary thought. So much had changed – I had changed and I had no idea how I would fit back into my previous life.

I was talking to a friend and she asked me: "How does it feel to be going back?" In that moment, I realised that it didn't feel too good to be 'going back'. Realising that that wasn't motivating, I opted to see it as 'moving on' to somewhere new and that felt exciting. I made the decision then not to return to London and instead to live somewhere new, to create a new life again, just like I had when I left London for Melbourne.

I started to consider different places to live in the UK, but I found the process difficult, as I just couldn't decide where I wanted to be. Having spent three years studying the power of the mind and visioning in particular, I spent one evening getting clear in my mind about what I really wanted. One of the things I loved the most about living in Melbourne was being in a city right by the sea. Every day, I would see the water and often a friend and I would walk the four kilometres along the promenade in the evenings. Out of everything, that was the thing about my life in Melbourne that I felt I would miss the most and so I realised in that moment that living by the sea was something I strongly desired.

I had also become used to living in houses as opposed to flats and much preferred it and so I added that to my list of 'wants'. I also wanted to set up my own therapy practice and living in a city was desirable if I was going to build a successful business, so I added that to my list also. At no point did I consider 'how' I was going to achieve any of this, or even if it was realistic. I had no plan. But I had intent.

I began to share these 'wants' with my family and friends, and about a week later an old family friend called me. She was about to get married and move to Canada and she had heard that I was planning to return to the UK. She wanted to know if I would be interested in renting her house. I had visited there once before and so I knew that she lived in a small town in South Wales but that was all. I asked her how far it was from Cardiff, the main city, and she told me it was a 10-minute drive. I then asked her if it was by the sea to which she replied that it was a 10-minute stroll to the pier. She told me more of her plans and her dates fitted in with mine perfectly. We went to end the call and she said, "Have a think and let me know". I was about to say, "Okay" before I realised that I had nothing to think about. My vision was of a house in a city by the sea and whilst I'd not considered moving to Wales, here I was being offered one. So, I accepted there and then.

Whether you believe that my intent played any part in the offer being made or not, it's undeniable that when the offer was made, my intent played a huge part in my accepting it, ticking a box and taking one step closer towards my vision.

When I ask people what they want their business to be, I get a variety of responses. Some are very clear on what they want and others are less so. For those who find it difficult, I tend to reframe the question and instead of asking them what they want, I ask them to imagine that they already have it. This is because, when you allow yourself to imagine enjoying 'success' as if it's already happening for real, your subconscious mind fills in the details for you based on your subconscious desires.

Remember, it's about what you **want**, not what you **don't want**. One of the most common reasons people don't achieve what they want is that their focus is on what they don't want in an attempt to avoid it. When you focus on the thing you don't want, your mind doesn't know that your intention is to avoid having it. All it knows is that you are directing it to that outcome and so your thoughts, feelings and behaviours become aligned with the very thing you want to avoid. There is a saying that describes this perfectly: "What you resist will persist". In order to resist something, you **have** to focus on it, and remember – you get what you focus on.

I worked with a client who was operating in his business overdraft month by month for six months before we started working together. His focus was on getting out of his overdraft and so, every month, he looked at, talked about and dreamed about his overdraft. His mind was so focused on resisting his overdraft that the existence of it persisted. Just one coaching session had him focusing on a positive bank balance at the end of that first month. It changed his perspective and because the plan of action we created was aligned with that outcome, a positive bank balance was exactly what he created, enabling him to invest in his business and to generate more revenue.

So, you don't want to stop procrastinating – you **want** to be more productive. You don't want to work with less of a particular type of client – you **want** to work with more of another type of client. You don't want to not have to worry about the payroll every month – you **want** to trigger the payroll a day or two earlier than necessary – because you can!

Focusing on what you want is important. But focusing on what you want is only the first step. You also have to focus on actually having it too. When you focus on having something as if it's happening right now, your subconscious mind and your behaviour is directed towards it. And this is *attractive.* However, there is a caveat to this: your focus on actually having it must be to the extent that it creates the positive feelings you associate with having it in order for it to really be effective. Let me explain:

The feeling of wanting something can manifest in two ways:

Our mind is focused on the thing we want and we become aware of what it looks and feels like when we have it. We feel **excited** and **motivated.**

Our mind is focused on the thing we want and we become aware of our current lack of it. We feel **miserable** and **anxious.**

The first reaction creates thoughts, feelings and sensations that make us feel good, and when we feel good we are in a space where we are able to appreciate what we already have and operate from a point of **gratitude** and **positivity**. The second reaction creates thoughts, feelings and sensations that make us feel bad, and when we feel bad we are unable to appreciate what we have now and we begin to operate from a point of **lack** and **negativity**. The first reaction is *attractive*, but the second reaction is the more common one and it explains why some people tend to focus on the thing they are trying to avoid, because focusing on what they are trying to achieve reminds them that they don't have it.

So, the key here is to focus on what you want without allowing your entire state of being to become so wrapped up in that future outcome, that it impedes your ability to enjoy the pursuit of it, and therefore your ability to achieve it.

Intimate relationships are a good example of this. Many people find their partner when they have given up on love. That's because they become 'unattached' to the outcome: whilst they may still 'desire' a relationship, they are not experiencing negative thoughts, feelings and sensations every time they think about relationships.

Someone I knew many years ago had this exact experience. She was (and still is) a very kind-hearted woman with lots to offer, who was desperate to meet the man of her dreams and settle down. This is true of many people, but for her, it was up there right at the top of her list of desirables. She talked about it all the time and often said things like "When I meet 'the one', then I will be happy". She woke every morning thinking about it and went to bed every night thinking about it. She often said she felt lonely. Whenever we went out as a group, the sight of couples canoodling would send her into a very sad place. Even without the knowledge I have now, I was aware that her belief that finding 'the one' was the sole answer to her entire future happiness was a) unrealistic and b) potentially getting in the way of her actually finding him. Her acute awareness of not having what she wanted made her feel resentful, so she would get drunk and lash out at her friends. Her behaviour was off-putting for men (and women!) and so she didn't attract the attention she wanted which impacted negatively on her self-esteem. The couple of relationships she did have were abusive which added to her low self-esteem. It was the opposite of *attractive.*

I didn't see her for a few years and when I next heard from her, it was by email to ask for my address as she wanted to send me an invitation – to her wedding. We talked on the phone and she shared with me that she had got so tired of looking for 'the one' and of feeling abused, that she gave up on love completely and threw herself into her work. That job led to an opportunity to work with children with special needs, something she had thought she might like to do, but had never pursued because her focus was on finding a relationship. The job was so rewarding and the value she added so evident that she began to believe in her own worth. The result was that she attracted the man she later married, into her life.

When you are able to want something, imagine what it's like to have it, and enjoy the feelings that go with that, you are able to enjoy what you have now and are more likely to attract what you want to you.

Just try it now. Imagine that your business is exactly as you want it to be right now. That's right, RIGHT NOW. Is it easy for you? Do the details of your ideal business come to mind with ease? If they do, then perhaps you already think about your business in this way. If this is a significant challenge (and it isn't easy for everyone), then relax, ACTivity 1 in The ACT Of ATTRACT section on page 67 will guide you through it.

PURPOSE (your 'why')

Purpose in this context essentially means 'reason'. It's your 'why'.

Whilst intent is about what you want to achieve, purpose is about your reason to do so which is infinitely more motivating. Purpose plays a significant role in your vision and because it leverages your 'why', it is far stronger than intent.

People are not driven by what they do, they are driven by **why** they do what they do. In other words, they are driven by the results that what they do delivers for them, and what those results mean to them. It's an emotional thing.

The power of 'why' cannot be overestimated: it can literally transform your life and business, because it provides the inspiration to take action (even when you don't feel like it), it gives you the strength to overcome challenges and it provides you with the drive and motivation to do the things necessary to create the result you want.

In my experience, the biggest reason people fail to achieve their goals is not because of a lack of knowledge of how to do so, but rather because of the lack of a strong enough reason to do so.

Think about this for a minute. Can you recall a time in your life when you set yourself a goal... you felt really excited about it... you probably took some action towards achieving it... and you possibly even made some progress... However, over time, your drive and energy dissipated and you found yourself looking back weeks later having not made the progress you intended. I can recall many times like this in my own life. People make decisions to change something in their life or business every single day. Often they understand exactly what steps they need to take to make it happen and yet often, they fail to do those things.

I would bet that those things you've wanted to do and haven't done are because you've either not taken enough action or you've not taken the right kind of action, and if that's true, then it's likely to be because you've not created a powerful enough reason to do so.

Now recall a time when you set yourself a goal and you achieved it. Perhaps you can recall lots of times like this? I know I can. What was different about those two scenarios? What was it that made one a success and the other a failure? What was it about the successful scenarios that made you so determined to succeed? If you look closely, you'll discover that the successes had something in common – a strong reason. That's the power of 'why'.

Often when we decide to make a change, we feel motivated to do it initially, but soon that motivation wanes because we forget 'why' we wanted it in the first place.

Remember, an attractive vision is one that motivates action and 'why' is and will always be your strongest motivator. Therefore, when designing your attractive vision, the single most powerful thing you can do to ensure that you achieve it, is to define your 'why' so that you have a significant enough reason to do so – one that has high emotional value to you – and then to remind yourself of it every single day. This is why purpose plays such a huge part in vision.

Discovering your purpose

The purpose aspect of vision often stems from our personal values, which put simply are the things that are important to us. So, to discover your purpose, it's important for you to focus on what's important to you about achieving the things you want to achieve.

Our values are usually based on ethical principles and they are our deepest driving force because they give everything we do meaning. This is why unless our life and our work are in line with them, we are often not inspired by them and motivated to take action.

Intent is about knowing 'what' you want your business to be like. Purpose is about knowing 'why' you want that. It's about what that outcome means to you and what you value specifically about that outcome.

Having been a planner from a young age, I went completely the other way when I had my 'mid-life crisis' at 29 (read my story at the back of the book) and stopped planning completely. Having previously managed to plan myself into being miserable, I replaced my 'what' and 'how' type goals with two very simple 'why' type goals. At that time, what was most important to me about my work was working with people I liked and doing what I was passionate about. I'd had the high salary, the nice car and the Chelsea pad and none of it had made me happy. So instead, I designed a vision almost entirely around those two simple values. They served as qualifiers whenever an opportunity arose: I would simply ask myself "Do I like them?" and "Am I passionate about it?" If the answer was yes, then I did it and if the answer was no, then I didn't. The result was that life became very simple. I found myself doing the things that I most enjoyed and was energised by, and with people I really liked, and I found myself selling my property and living, working and studying in Australia. When I returned to the UK from Melbourne, and was faced with starting a business in a town where I knew literally nobody, those two values continued to serve me well. They enabled me to make decisions about which opportunities to take (and which not to take) with ease, and I credit them with the success I experienced in my life and my businesses.

There are many values you can hold and the order of priority you place on those values will determine your approach to your business.

You might value recognition or accolade. You might value integrity. You might value financial freedom, or creativity, or being the first to achieve something. You might value a specific change in your industry or profession, or you might value being known as a 'change maker'. What you value most might simply be the joy of interacting with a particular type of person or client.

Remember, having a strong emotional connection to your 'why' will do more for your motivation and therefore your results than just about anything else.

Think about it now. What is it about your intent, in other words, the things you want to achieve that is so important to you? What is it about not having those things that is so uncomfortable? What will your life look like when you achieve them? What will your life look like if you don't? How will it impact on your family or friends when you do have it? How will they suffer if you don't do it?

Again, this may come really easily to you and if it does, that's great. However, it may not be quite so easy, and whatever the case, relax for now, ACTivity 1 in The ACT Of ATTRACT section on page 67 will guide you through it.

Creating your *attractive* vision

Once you have determined your intent and your purpose, you have the basis of an *attractive* vision.

However, you want your vision to exist as reality at some point in the future, which means that you need it to inspire you and motivate you to take action. It's true that the more clarity there is around your vision, the more inspired you will feel, the more likely it is that you will start to envisage the path ahead and the more motivated you will be to do what's necessary to make it reality. However, an *attractive* vision is most powerful when it exists in some tangible form (outside of your head) because when your vision is tangible (as well as clear), it becomes more **ACT**ionable and remember this is The **ACT** Of Attraction!

Think of creating a tangible vision as literally creating your future history, in other words, creating the outcome as if it exists NOW. The purpose of this is that when your vision exists in some form other than in your imagination, your subconscious mind starts to fully embrace it and to believe it is real, and once it starts to do that, it will direct your behaviour to that which is conducive to making it so.

There are many ways to create your future history. It might suit you to write or type it up, or you might create a montage of images that depict the details of your vision. You might record yourself or someone else speaking it, or you might commit it to video. The method you choose is entirely up to you.

Whatever method you choose, an *attractive* vision that is also actionable is one that evokes all of the senses: sight, sound, smell, taste and touch. This is because the subconscious mind, which is responsible for our behaviour, is stimulated through the senses.

Some people are more stimulated through some senses than others and it helps to leverage the ones that work most for you. For instance, some people are more visual than others, which means that they have a preference for things that can be seen or observed, like pictures and diagrams or videos and presentations. These people say things like: "I see what you mean". Some people are more auditory, which means that they have a preference for things that can be heard, like sounds and the spoken word. They say things like: "Tell me about it", or "I hear you".

And, other people are more kinaesthetic, which means that they have a preference for physical experience, like touching, feeling, holding and doing. They say things like: "I sense that", or "Let me have a go".

Your choice of method of creating your attractive actionable vision will be driven by your own preference, which is why I have included two options here for you so that you can choose the one that suits you (you might even choose to do both!).

Remember, you are designing the future of your business, and design by definition is a creative activity. Whichever method you choose, creating your vision is intended to be a relaxing and enjoyable experience, and, as the result of it is so incredibly important to your *attraction*, you will want to make sure that you organise your environment so that you have ample space and time to do it justice.

Your Vision Board

A Vision Board is a collection of images that portray the details of your vision: who you want to be, what you want to achieve, what you want to own, where you want to live or travel and who you want in your life. A Vision Board is perfect for highly visual people.

When you surround yourself with images that depict the things you desire, and that are most important to you, it creates the feelings that go with that and an internal mental image of that outcome so that your thinking and your behaviour changes to match that desire and those images. Your intent really is that powerful.

The images can be a combination of very specific ones: places, buildings and people, and images that simply evoke a feeling: a picture of something that makes you feel a certain way.

There are lots of different ways to create a vision board. You can use a large (A3 or bigger) piece of cardboard and glue images onto it to make a collage – the images can be cut out of magazines, or printed from the internet. You can create a wallpaper for your computer from images that you have downloaded from the internet, or you can create a collage on your computer and print it off to put on your wall. You can even draw the images if you're artistic (I tried this once and my white

Audi TT looked more like a VW Beetle, so I opted for a printed image!). How you do it is up to you.

I remember my first vision board vividly. I created it soon after I watched 'The Secret' by Rhonda Byrne. I was so inspired by that film that I set about creating my vision with excitement. I remember it had a picture of a plane and the Sydney Harbour Bridge, as I was keen to get back to Australia to see my friends. It had a white Audi TT, the car of my dreams, and it had an image of an audience, as I was keen to continue training. It had a bank statement with the balance doctored to show a healthy income. I placed it to the right of my desk in my office where I could see it every day and whilst I did not look at it daily, I was always aware of its presence. That vision board featured the things I 'wanted' at that time in my life, and whilst some things took longer than others, most aspects of that vision board occurred during the following year (the Audi took three!).

If you have chosen the Vision Board option to document your vision, then ACTivity 2 in The ACT Of ATTRACT section on page 77 will guide you through it.

Your Provocative Proposition

A Provocative Proposition is a written account of your life and business in the future as if it is happening right now: who you are, what you've achieved, what you own, where you live or travel and who you have in your life. It is great for people who are more kinaesthetic and it works well for people who also have a visual and/or auditory preference.

Its intention is to put the desired outcome at a conscious level whilst also directing the subconscious mind towards it. It is 'provocative' to the extent that it intentionally stretches the scope of the current situation, challenges limiting beliefs and represents your desired outcome as if it is real.

When you describe your vision in detail as if it's already happening, it generates the feelings that go with that so that your thinking and your behaviour change to match that reality.

The beauty of a provocative proposition is that it provides two important motivators: the 'big picture' (visual) and the detail, including sounds (auditory), and it is written in the present tense as if you are already there, living that reality (kinaesthetic).

Like a vision board, when you write your future history as an account of a day in the future, as if it's already happened, you create the images (visual), sounds (auditory), feelings and sensations (kinaesthetic) that go with that account. This creates an internal reality of the outcome and your thinking and behaviour changes to match that reality. Your intent really is that powerful.

Your Provocative Proposition describes a day in your life at some point in the future (at least 12 months away) from the minute you wake up until just before you sleep. It portrays your life and your business as it is on that day based on your vision. It is written in the present tense and using full sensory language, i.e. language that evokes all the senses: sight, smell, sound (auditory), taste and touch.

I have written a number of Provocative Propositions in the past and I have had the privilege of working with many others on theirs. The one I wrote back in July 2008 when I was practising as a therapist in a small town in South Wales described my life and my business in detail.

Whilst I was really enjoying working one on one with clients and was seeing some incredible results, I felt very limited in the impact I could have. I maintained my strong desire to impact the development of people en masse, but I couldn't see how I could do that using my combined HR, leadership, psychology and hypnosis skills. I had been drawn, in my corporate days, to roles where I could positively influence people's lives, and whilst I had no desire to work in the corporate world again, I was still very passionate about people development and I was also developing a passion for business.

So, I wrote in this Provocative Proposition about the work I was doing within an organisation that was genuinely concerned with people development. I wasn't specific about what I was doing, but I was specific about how much I was enjoying what I was doing, and why, and I was specific about the people I was working with and how grateful I felt to be playing a significant part in it. Little did I know at that time that I would later play a pivotal role in creating a National Business Network with a personal and business development platform. I remember reading this Provocative Proposition a year or so later and how amazed I was at how accurate the description was of the role I was now playing. Even with the knowledge I had about the power of intent and the belief I had in attraction, I was blown away.

Your Provocative Proposition is designed to evoke all your senses so that the day in the future that you have created is fully experienced as if it were real. As a result, it becomes real in your subconscious mind and as you now know, that means it's real!

Your attention is incredibly powerful, so it's important that you do not simply put your Provocative Proposition in a drawer, never to be seen again. Read it occasionally and fully immerse yourself in it when you do, as by doing so, you will be motivated to do the things necessary to make it happen.

If you have chosen the Provocative Proposition option to document your vision, then ACTivity 2 in The ACT Of ATTRACT section on page 77 will guide you through it.

Engage others in your vision

You may have heard the saying: "If you want to achieve something, tell others". The rationale is that telling others creates the accountability you need to follow through. For instance, if your goal is to run the London marathon and you tell your friends that you are going to do it, it is highly likely that they will ask you about it as you get closer. I know many people who have done just that. This kind of accountability can be very motivating.

There is another perspective on this though. Telling others about your goal makes it less likely to happen, because the approval you receive creates an affirmative satisfaction of achieving the goal, without having to actually do the work. Your *talking* becomes a substitute for *doing*.

Whilst this goes against conventional goal-setting, it does make some sense and there is a valid argument for both.

However, in a business context, I feel strongly that you must engage the people who are in, contribute to, or are affected by your business in your vision. Whether you are a single practitioner business, or an owner of a larger business, you are the leader and it is your role to define the direction of the business and to engage your team in that vision to ensure that you (and they) achieve it.

I recommend sharing your vision with the people who have a vested interest in your success. This includes your team (if you have one) but it also includes your partner, your parents, your children, your suppliers, your coach or mentor and possibly even your clients. In order to ensure that they are fully engaged, make sure that you share both your *intent* and your *purpose.* Different elements will resonate with different people.

By engaging other people in your vision, you make it more real, and you commit to it on a whole different level!

Engaging others in the business vision is something I have done a number of times. In a previous role, whilst as a board, we came up with the overall vision for the business, our senior management team were fully engaged in the process. This not only ensured their buy-in and secured their commitment, but it also meant that they held each other accountable for each other's results. These days, I run a much smaller business, but I have a number of associates, many suppliers and a mentor, all of whom are fully involved in my vision for the business. It means that everything that gets done is done with the bigger picture in mind and everyone understands the role they play in making it happen. It gives even the smallest of tasks meaning and a sense of satisfaction for all involved.

YOUR MIND-SET

Once you've got a vision so you know where you are going and you have a daily reminder to keep you on track, you've got half of the ATTRACT element covered!

To complete the 'internal activity' aspect of The Act Of Attraction, you need an *attractive* mind-set, and an *attractive* mind-set is specifically one that conditions you internally for success.

Our success is influenced greatly by the mind-set we hold. What we believe, what we think and how we feel, dictates how we perceive and respond to situations. Like attracts like and so our beliefs, thoughts and feelings determine the reality we experience.

For example, if our mind is occupied with thoughts and expectations of struggle and problems, then we perceive struggle and problems and that perspective means that we attract struggle and problems to our lives. Conversely, if our mind is occupied with thoughts and expectations of success and happiness, then success and happiness is what we attract.

Put simply, an *attractive* mind-set is a positive one. The word 'positive' means to *affirm* or to be *certain*, and mind-set is essentially about *attitude* and *intent*. So, to have a positive mind-set is to *affirm* with *intent* and your positivity has real intent when it's aligned with your vision.

People with a positive mind-set have beliefs that support their vision, which means that their thoughts are affirmative and their feelings are ones of certainty. They are self-led, which means that they take responsibility for their own life and success and they have a high level of self-awareness, which enables them to identify unattractive thoughts and behaviours easily and replace them quickly with *attractive* ones.

I work with a lot of people in business who have a passion for what they do and who understand intellectually the power of a positive mind-set. However, there is a difference between understanding the power of it intellectually and having the ability to create it so that you attract into your life the things that you want.

Positive thinking

Clearly there is tremendous power in thinking positively – the more positive our thoughts, the better we feel and the more bright and promising life looks. However, the ability to think positively does not constitute a positive mind-set. A positive mind-set is a predominant mental attitude where your beliefs, thoughts and feelings are aligned with your vision (what you want and why). What happens then is that in addition to having a sense of certainty and feeling confident, your subconscious behaviour also becomes naturally aligned with your intent and purpose so that you begin to *attract* to you the people and the opportunities that will enable you to move forwards towards the outcome you intend with ease. This is what I mean by an *attractive* mind-set in the context of The Act Of Attraction.

The more affirmative your mind-set, the more powerful it'll be and the more it'll support you in the achievement of your goals. However, your mind-set does not need to be rock-solid in order for you to attract the things that will enable your success.

Even the most successful business people have self-doubt and fears – it's all part of being human. We are all evolving continually, and arguably we never reach 100% unwavering belief.

My self-belief is not bullet-proof (and I teach this stuff!). There have been times in my life when I have felt completely tuned in and confident – like I could take on the world. And there have been times when I have felt I suddenly lacked the personal resources I needed to achieve something. Sometimes we fail and it takes some time to lick our wounds and learn the lesson before we can get back on our line. Sometimes something completely outside of our control happens that knocks us off track and it requires a whole new way of thinking, or behaving, to get us back on track. Sometimes we just inexplicably have a bad day. It's what makes life interesting and sometimes it's the very thing that propels us on to achieve more.

I believe that we need the moments of darkness in our lives in order to fully appreciate the moments of lightness. There is no night without day and there is no positivity without the opposite. It's also true that self-doubt is not always negative. Of course it is when it's constant and it consistently gets in our way, but a little bit of self-doubt can be healthy – it can keep us grounded and it can give us something to kick against, creating the momentum we need to move forward.

The mind-set piece is therefore not about creating such a bullet-proof mind-set that you'll never experience any doubt or waver in your belief for ever more. What it is about is becoming aware of the different components that make up mind-set, spending some time self-reflecting to identify what specifically needs to change, and then applying some conscious effort to make changes that will result in a mind-set that supports you in the pursuit of your vision.

For some, this is the most challenging part of The Act Of Attraction. However, like anything, if you really want something, and you have a strong enough 'why', you need to make it a priority and give it the appropriate attention. You need to choose voluntarily to apply conscious effort in the short-term in order to gain long-term benefit and this means consciously and consistently taking actions that might not be usual for you. Remember, everyone has doubts and fears, even successful people. The only difference between successful people and unsuccessful people is that successful people push through theirs.

Creating your *attractive* mind-set is dependent on developing two things: *1. Self-Leadership* and *2. Self-Conditioning.*

SELF-LEADERSHIP

Self-Leadership is the commitment and the capacity to take responsibility for and create your own success. It is the ability to influence and guide yourself and it is the opposite of shifting responsibility for your success onto other people or circumstances. This means both acknowledging and accepting that you are responsible for your own life – that ultimately it's down to YOU.

The people who make drastic transformations in their business do so as a result of accepting and embracing self-responsibility. Self-responsibility means considering yourself to be the 'creator' of your life as opposed to the 'receiver' of it. It means owning your decisions and being answerable for the implications of those decisions and it means owning your reactions to people and to circumstances. The importance of this mental shift cannot be overstated.

Self-responsibility can be very uncomfortable because it essentially means taking the blame for whatever isn't right in your life, and let's face it – it's much more comfortable to do the opposite!

We've all used blame to get us off the hook. We've blamed our parents for the way we think, or our partner for the way we feel. Some people even manage to blame others for what they themselves have done! Only a few weeks ago, a client of mine told me that the reason she hadn't completed a task she'd committed to completing was that her mother was disorganised!

Whilst blaming other people or circumstances for the things that go wrong in our lives might feel more comfortable as it absolves us of responsibility, it rarely results in the outcome we want.

When you take responsibility, you claim power over your life which gives you freedom to make of it whatever you want, and whilst taking responsibility may not always be comfortable, it is very liberating as it gives you choice over what you believe, think and feel, and in effect, what you do.

I learned this in 2001 when I realised that despite achieving all my goals, I was miserable. I'd literally planned myself into a job I hated and a life that I was enjoying less and less, because I'd not invested time in defining my intent and purpose.

I learned it again when I found myself, after investing nearly five years in building a business, becoming increasingly unhappy with some of the things that were happening around me. After weeks of feeling trapped, angry and resentful and trying desperately to influence the behaviour of other people, I simply accepted that I was not responsible for their actions and only responsible for my own. What resulted from that was immense clarity and a significant decision, and whilst what followed wasn't particularly pleasant, I ultimately created the space and the freedom to attract the people and the circumstances that I actually want in my business and in my life.

As well as having self-responsibility, people who are self-led have a high level of self-awareness. Self-awareness is simply about understanding ourselves better. The better and the more deeply we know ourselves, the more we are able to influence and guide ourselves effectively. This means being aware of our current conditioning and understanding what it is that makes us who we are.

The first step is noticing and examining our beliefs and how they manifest in our thoughts, feelings and behaviours. Once we are aware of the beliefs we hold, we can begin to make the necessary adjustments to those beliefs to enable us to be more purposeful in our behaviour.

As I said earlier, this is not always comfortable. Many of us have been conditioned to believe that we are fundamentally flawed, which makes looking at ourselves unappealing – terrifying even. However, the truth is that without identifying where you are right now, it is not possible to make the changes to your mind-set so that it supports you in the pursuit of your vision.

Your beliefs are governing your life!

Our beliefs are formed through a direct auto-suggestive process during childhood and are held at a subconscious level. They provide a framework for both our conscious decisions and our behaviour. Whilst as adults, we have the ability to assess the information that we receive and to choose to accept or reject it, as children, we lacked that critical analytical ability. Information was not considered, and instead, it was simply accepted, without question. These autosuggestions then formed the foundation of the beliefs upon which all subsequent beliefs were and are formed; our perception of ourselves as individuals and the level of worth we consider we have in the world, and the subsequent attitude and behaviour with which we approach our daily lives.

How this conditioning manifests in our beliefs can be best understood by looking at the two fundamental aspects of self-belief: self-esteem and self-efficacy.

Self-esteem is our general sense of the value we have in the world. The word 'esteem' originates from a Latin word that means 'to estimate', so, self-esteem is how we estimate ourselves. This often comes from an awareness of the contribution we make to the lives of those around us as well as a general feeling that they approve of us.

People with low self-esteem do not hold themselves in high regard and therefore do not consider that they are deserving of love, happiness or success. They tend to beat themselves up when they make a mistake and to feel that they are 'no good' if something negative happens in their life. They respond by acting in a self-defeating or self-destructive manner and their behaviour tends to be predominantly automatic.

People with healthy self-esteem regard themselves favourably and consider that they are worthy of love, happiness and success. They do not define their entire being based on their occasional failures and instead accept that mistakes are simply part of the deal. They live more consciously, aware of themselves, and their reactions.

Self-efficacy relates to our perception of our ability to learn, to develop skills and to apply ourselves to achieve a result. It affects our social interactions in almost every way.

People with low self-efficacy will resist pursuing opportunities or accepting challenges because they do not believe they have the ability to succeed, regardless of their effort. People with healthy self-efficacy will accept challenges readily, and they will work harder and persist longer when they encounter difficulties.

Both self-esteem and self-efficacy are important aspects of self-belief and often when one is lacking, the other is too.

Whatever our subconscious beliefs are, our thoughts and feelings are intrinsically linked to them. Our behaviour, both internal and external, is then a by-product of those beliefs, which explains why sometimes what we do does not reflect what we desire.

What we believe is what we achieve, so recognising the link between beliefs, thoughts and feelings and behaviour is an important first step in making the adjustments to our belief systems that enable us to develop behaviour that is more conducive to achieving the things that make us happy and successful. The second step is identifying what they are.

Your thoughts are your beliefs in action

The best indicator of the belief systems you hold in your mind is the thoughts you have.

Another way to describe the thoughts you have is 'self-talk'. Self-talk is the dialogue you have inside your own head. Many people are barely aware of their self-talk as it's so automatic (a bit like the auto-suggestion I mentioned earlier), and others are acutely aware of it. However, the extent to which you are aware of your self-talk has no bearing on its impact on the way you feel and the way you behave.

Now, you may be thinking: "What's she on about? I don't have voices in my head!" Yes, you do. That was one right there!

I used to do lots of talks on the power of the mind when I was running my therapy business, and when I got to the part about self-talk, I would ask the audience to put their hand up if they knew what I was talking about. Whilst half the room would put their hand up straight away, some would sit looking at me blankly and others would shake their head. No matter who I looked at, I could almost see the internal dialogue going on: "I have no idea what you mean", "I don't talk to myself", "I'm not admitting that, that'd make me look crazy". At that point I'd say, "For those of you without your hands up, thinking 'I don't have self-talk'... it's that thought right there!!"

You see – everyone has self-talk. Self-talk is not only normal; it is an essential part of the process of evaluating and processing information. Each and every day, our mind is bombarded with suggestions: the things we do, see, hear, taste and touch; the people we interact with and the things they do and say; the stuff we read, etc. Our mind has to disseminate that information and make sense of it and our thoughts are part of that process.

So, the only difference between those who say they don't have self-talk and those who say they do, is that those who say they don't are unaware of theirs. The only people who don't have self-talk are dead people (and that would be debated by some!).

Once you start to become aware of what you are saying to yourself, you will have a better understanding of the belief systems you hold, and once you know what they are, you can choose which ones to keep and which ones to lose.

The key to becoming aware of your belief systems is to intentionally tune into your internal voice and be aware of what it is saying to you and the feelings it generates. Admittedly, this is easier for some than others, but most people find that when they apply themselves consciously to listening for their internal dialogue, they start to become aware of it almost immediately.

The times when you are most likely to be aware of your self-talk are times when you are on autopilot. You know, those times when you are just 'doing' without thinking. Like showering, or driving, or sitting on the loo! When I first started to become aware of my self-talk, I would notice it when I was waiting for the kettle to boil, or listening to 'on hold' music on the phone, or waiting for a bus. This is because the conscious mind is not 'doing' anything and so your mind is in what's known as an 'altered state'. It's in this state that your self-talk is most evident.

Your self-talk can be like a helpful coach who believes in you: supporting and encouraging you, inspiring affirmative feelings in you and resulting in positive action. Or, it can be like a bully: undermining and criticising you, resulting in demotivation and self-destructive behaviour.

Some people are not surprised by what they discover when they tune into their self-talk, whilst others are very surprised. Whatever the case, having this awareness is crucial as it provides an essential explanation for the things we currently have in our life.

Your self-talk is creating your reality

There's a saying: "What you think about, you bring about". What this means is that your thoughts literally become things. This is because thoughts generate feelings and both are responsible for behaviour. If you have goals, but you are not achieving them, the chances are you have beliefs that are in conflict with them, and this will inevitably be showing up as negative self-talk.

Negative self-talk is essentially thoughts that lead you to feel negative. That's because negative thoughts create stress. For example, if you tell yourself that something you need to deal with will be 'difficult', then your body responds to that thought with the appropriate feelings, as the body starts to prepare itself for difficulty. Whilst the good news is that this means that your body is working properly (it is providing you with the resources you need to deal with the situation), it is responding to a perceived threat that is not real. If you were to view the same situation as a 'positive challenge' or 'an opportunity for learning' for instance, then your body would respond to that thought with feelings that are appropriate to dealing with that. Whilst still preparing you, it is preparing you with the resources that will enable you to deal with a challenge or an opportunity, as opposed to facing difficulty.

The difference may seem subtle, but the impact is significant. Negative thoughts that are left to run their course manifest in negative outcomes. It's a bit like the worrying analogy I used earlier, if we perceive that something is going to be a certain way and we prepare physiologically for that outcome, the chances are we will manifest it. Self-talk is self-fulfilling – always, so the more positive it is, the better.

SELF-CONDITIONING

If self-leadership is the commitment and the capacity to take responsibility for our own success, then self-conditioning is the conscious application of that in creating an *attractive* mind-set to enable that success to become reality.

Whilst it is true that we have been conditioned up to this point based on past experiences and that our behaviour is driven by that conditioning, that does not mean that we have no control over any of it.

In fact, the opposite is true. Think about it – if your mind has been conditioned once, it makes sense that it can be conditioned again, doesn't it? The truth is that your current intent is stronger than your historic beliefs and if you have a strong enough desire to change your beliefs and you believe that you can, then you can, and you will.

Remember, an attractive mind-set is a positive mind-set – to affirm with intent. That means creating a strong sense of certainty in relation to your vision through the generation of affirmative thoughts that are focused around the outcome you want.

It sounds simple, and it is, but that doesn't mean it's easy. It requires attention and conscious effort initially to create 'desired internal behaviour' that will eventually become habitual, and manifest in desired external behaviour.

It's not a one hit shot either. There are no quick fixes in mind-set shifting – remember, it took years to create the one you have now. However, the good news is that it won't take years to create the one you want as you now have wisdom and resources that you lacked back then.

So, as we explore the different facets of mind-set with the intent to change yours where necessary, don't expect to get it right first time – you won't. Just aim to get it right for right now.

Creating your *attractive* mind-set

Once you have a vision for your business and you have awareness of the beliefs you hold that don't support it, you need to create an attractive mind-set in order to attract it. This is what self-conditioning is all about – choosing what your predominant mental attitude will be and then actively seeking to create it.

You are the gatekeeper!

I liken mind-set to a garden. You can have a beautiful garden that you created yourself which features all the qualities of your choice: one that you're proud of and that makes you feel good, that you want to hang out in and invite people into. Or, you can have a garden that was created by other people and circumstances, over many years.

It's a very powerful analogy as the mind finds it easy to relate to the nature aspect of it. I used to use it a lot when working with hypnosis with clients with low confidence or self-esteem. I would take them through a process where they would imagine walking around their own mind-set garden, which was filled with the results of all their old conditioning. They would pay attention to the old dried-up leaves, bits of debris and toxic weeds and while doing so, they would allow images or memories of the people or circumstances that those objects represented to come to mind. When we do this, the subconscious mind attaches those beliefs, thoughts, feelings and memories to the object of our attention and so whatever we then do with that object, it literally does with the belief or feeling.

Remember, the subconscious doesn't know the difference between real or imagined, and if you imagine something vividly, you create a neurological pathway in your mind in exactly the same way as if you do it for real. So, when they then imagined sweeping all of the old outdated negative and unhelpful conditioning into a pile and burning it, their subconscious mind literally rid itself of the relevant beliefs, etc.

Later they would imagine planting new seeds for the things they wanted in their life like confidence, calm, success...

The reason I mention this is that creating the mind-set you want starts with planting the seeds for the beliefs you want to have. But it doesn't end there. You have to then nurture the seeds just like your old outdated beliefs were nurtured, so that they become as effective at directing your future behaviour as the old beliefs were at directing your old behaviour. Within time, the seeds will sprout and little shoots will grow beneath the surface, eventually manifesting above the surface in what you say and do.

The message here is that **you** are the gatekeeper to your mind. You choose what you let in and what you keep and you also choose what you let go of. Additionally, you choose what you let into your life: the environment that you create around you, the people you hang out with, the stuff you watch, read and listen to.

So, taking the garden analogy, what seeds will you plant for the success you want to create? What beliefs will you plant to support you in achieving it?

The saying 'thoughts become things' applies to beliefs too. One of the most powerful ways to change your beliefs is to change your thoughts. Remember, your thoughts are directly linked to your beliefs, and whilst when you are operating automatically, your beliefs dictate your feelings, when you take control of your thoughts and feelings consciously, you are able to influence your beliefs dramatically.

Attractive thoughts are thoughts that lead to a desired belief or outcome and so by definition, they are thoughts that are framed in positive language. The power of language is often underestimated. Your choice of words can make a significant difference to the quality of your thoughts and, in fact, the way a thought is worded can be the difference between it having a positive or negative effect. For instance, the mind doesn't recognise statements that are framed in the negative as well as it does statements that are framed in the positive. So, when you think, "I don't want to fail", the mind doesn't easily recognise the intention **not** to fail as it is easier to recognise failing. If you think, "I want to succeed", that thought is far easier for the mind to recognise. This is especially true of children, and if you have children, you'll have seen this in action. Say to a child "don't run" and what do they do? That's because what they heard was 'run'. Tell a child to "walk please", and they are more likely to stop running.

Here's another example: Don't think about a blue door. Right now, **do not** think about a blue door. It's impossible isn't it? In order to not think about that blue door in your mind, you had to think about it first. Even if you are now thinking about a red car instead, your mind had to access the blue door first before you changed it to a red car. It's not possible 'not' to think about something. It is only possible to actively think about something different.

Creating your *attractive* beliefs

In an ideal world, you would be so aware of your negative self-talk that you would competently replace *unattractive* thoughts with *attractive* ones. However, in reality, it is not that easy. I would recommend dealing with the negative thoughts before seeking to replace them with positive ones. This is how:

1. Delete it

Consider that your mind is like a computer, which it essentially is. Now think of your self-talk as spam. What is spam? Spam is essentially unsolicited and indiscriminate email messages sent in an attempt to force information on people who don't want it. Sound familiar? Every day your computer is infiltrated by unwanted and unhelpful spam. You didn't ask for it, did you? And it's not of any use, is it? So, what do you do with spam? You delete it, right?

Well, imagine that you can do the same with the spam you receive into your mind. As you have a thought that is unattractive, you imagine in your mind a keyboard, and on that keyboard is a delete key. When you have a thought that is not *attractive*, imagine deleting that thought by literally pressing the delete key in your mind. The key (s'cuse the pun!) is to literally do the physical action of pressing the delete key. Remember, your mind does not know the difference between what's real and what's imagined and so your subconscious mind will believe that you have literally deleted that thought from your mind. When you delete the thought, you interrupt the process that would normally have occurred and so the feeling that would have followed doesn't and neither does the behaviour.

Please do try this. I used to do this myself years ago when my internal dialogue wasn't *attractive* and I still use it now if my internal thoughts are self-doubting, especially before I speak publicly. I also used to teach this at seminars and people would feedback to me that they would use it, and sometimes, after just a few conscious actions of deleting thoughts, the thoughts would cease completely. It works!

2. Replace it

Once you've mastered deleting negative thoughts, you will want to replace them with attractive ones.

There are two options here, you can either replace it, or reframe it.

Replace the negative thought with an affirming one: instead of trying to negate the negative in that thought, say the opposite instead. So, rather than "I am scared" becoming "I am not scared", it becomes "I am confident", or "I am courageous". Or, reframe it as a question. When a thought limits the possibilities of a given situation, turn it into a question. Rather than "I can't do this", change the thought to: "How can I do this?" The act of asking "how?" gets you into a creative, problem-solving mind-set, which means the subsequent thought is more likely to be positive.

Creating your *attractive* feelings

When you start to take control of how you think, you begin to positively affect how you feel too. However, whilst your feelings are directly linked to and influenced by your thoughts, you can also influence how you feel directly, by doing things that you know will generate the feelings you want.

One of my desired feelings is to feel connected. It's a basic human need to feel this way, but for me it is a 'core' need and it has driven much of what I have done in my life. In my personal life I have often attracted people with whom I have developed a deep bond quickly, and in my work I have favoured roles that have enabled me to connect at a deep level with people. In order to ensure that I meet that need in myself, I have surrounded myself with a number of people with whom I share a deep bond. When I sense the need to feel connected, I make contact with one of them.

Another feeling I crave is to feel useful. It stems from my desire to help people and so everything I do, both in business and in my life, is driven by that. Whilst my business is strategy focused, my content and my style of delivery is always with the intention of fulfilling the need to feel useful – in fact, this book is an example.

Similarly, I use music to create feelings I desire. If I am on my way to speak at an event, I play uplifting music that makes me smile and often I sing along at high volume as this fills me with happy endorphins, which I feel throughout my body. If I want to feel energised, I play music that makes me want to move. It's simple stuff, but it's also stuff that works.

Affirming your outcome

Remember, 'positive mind-set' means to 'affirm' with 'intent', and affirmations are a great tool for this. Affirmations are statements that describe an intended outcome in an affirmative way (with certainty) which when repeated frequently with real attention, literally transform the way you think and feel. This works in exactly the same way that negative self-talk does, but in a way that benefits you rather than hinders you.

The key to a powerful affirmation is for it to be framed in the 'now' and in positive language and for it to be consistently visible to you. If you place it where it is constantly visible (I have mine by my kettle and on my bedroom mirror), and where you will be confronted with it daily as a minimum, you will be reminded of it. Every time you see it and say it to yourself intentionally, both silently and out loud, you self-condition your own mind.

After a period of between 21 days and three months of consistent conscious effort, this statement will become embedded as part of your mind-set.

ACTivity 3 in The ACT Of ATTRACT section on page 81 will guide you through writing your affirmation.

Creating unquestionable evidence

The last part of the mind-set piece is concerned with convincing yourself of your capability and credibility.

Often when working with people to develop their business we get to the planning stage, or the stage where they actually have to go out and implement some of the plans, and suddenly the excitement is replaced with a whole lot of self-doubt. We are very good at convincing ourselves that we don't have the skills or the capability or the credibility to achieve something, even when we have done similar things before.

When someone else's credibility is in question, we tend to look for evidence of their work to convince ourselves that they can do the job. We read testimonials or we ask other people about them. The same approach works in conditioning our own mind about our own credibility. When I am working with someone and this issue arises, I get them to list their credibility factors: qualifications, experience, tangible outcomes, things they've written, things other people have said, etc, so that they bring into conscious awareness real evidence of their capability. This list can then be referred back to at times when they need to remind or convince themselves of their own credibility.

So, think about the evidence you have that backs up your new thoughts and beliefs. What experience do you have? What knowledge? What skills? What successes have you had? Your previous successes highlight your capabilities and your strengths and by bringing evidence of them into your conscious awareness now, you can strengthen your internal belief system. In doing so, you regenerate the feelings that go with that evidence, and when you feel a certain way, you act that way too which is *attractive*.

Identifying your strengths

Often, we think of our 'strengths' as being the things that we are good at. For me, a 'strength' is not just something that you do well, a strength is something that you do well, and that you **enjoy** doing. A strength is something that when you do it, it makes you feel stronger, because it energises you. It's often the thing that others notice about you and possibly even remark on and that you could do all day long without tiring.

I don't know about you, but I am good at lots of things that actually I don't particularly enjoy. For instance, I'm not bad with spreadsheets: I can create them, I can make them look pretty and I can make them calculate formulas, etc. I am also not bad at creating and writing business processes and I have done this for many businesses and continue to do so. However, if I am honest, neither of these things are things that energise me. If they were not necessary activities and they did not enable the results I want and that I **am** energised by, I would probably choose not to do them at all. I therefore don't consider these things my strengths.

What does make me feel energised and strong is working with business people on their vision and mind-set and helping them to create the behaviour and plan to drive their business forward. What I enjoy most is working with teams to create a shared vision, with common goals, and working with them to create roles and define responsibilities that enable each team member to play to their strengths. Those are my strengths.

So, what do you do that you are both good at, and that you enjoy? What have you done in your life that made you feel energised? What could you talk about or do for hours without tiring? And, what would you do even if you didn't get paid? **These are your real strengths.**

ACTivity 4 in The ACT Of ATTRACT section on page 89 will guide you through creating your unquestionable evidence.

The ACT Of ATTRACT (ACTivities)

Go to www.theactofattraction.com to download these worksheets

YOUR VISION

ACTIVITY 1:
DEFINE YOUR INTENT AND PURPOSE

Define your Intent and Purpose to ensure that your vision motivates you to take action

Remember, when you are able to want something, imagine what it's like to have it, and enjoy the feelings that go with that, you are able to enjoy what you have now and are more likely to attract it to you. This activity requires you to visualise yourself at a time in the future when your business and life is exactly as you want it to be, and it works best when you follow the steps, including the preparation.

Preparation

- o Find somewhere quiet and private to sit, or to lie down, and make sure you won't be disturbed.

- o Close your eyes and take some deep breaths in through your nose and out through your mouth.

- o Relax and allow your breathing to become rhythmic.

When you are completely relaxed:

- o Allow yourself to become aware of yourself in the future at a time when your business is exactly as you want it to be. If you don't know exactly what that is yet that's okay. Just imagine for now that it is happening and see what comes up.

- o Allow the feelings that come with having the business you want to come over you. Feel how it feels to have that business – to feel that success.

- o Hear the sounds that go with having that business and success: perhaps people are congratulating you? Perhaps there is music, or laughter?

o Now, become aware of the things you can see in that picture: it doesn't matter if you can't actually see images, whatever you are aware of, it is what it is: Where are you? Who is there? What's happening?

Open your eyes and complete worksheets 1 and 2. There are no ideal answers here. The only right answers are the ones that come to you right now, so just write what comes to mind. You may not even have an answer come to mind for every question and that's okay. The questions are there simply to guide you, and in fact, the questions for which you do have an answer arguably represent the areas that are most important to you, or where you have the strongest desire right now.

It is important that you write these down. It's not enough to simply 'think' them.

WORKSHEET 1	YOUR VISION – INTENT ('What' you want)

What kind of work are you doing?

Where are you doing it? This could be your location or your environment (or both).

What kind of clients/customers are you attracting?

What connections or relationships have you created?

What kind of people are you collaborating with?

Who are your team? This includes your coach, mentor, employees and suppliers.

What kind of support network do you have?

What kind of revenue are you generating?

What kind of person are you? What qualities do you have?

How do you interact with the people you work with and for?

What things do people say about you?

Where are you living?

What are you and your family enjoying most about your new lifestyle?

What activities are you doing outside of your business?

WORKSHEET 2   YOUR VISION – PURPOSE ('why' you want it)

On page 76 you will find a table of words that translate to values to help you.

What is it about your intent that is so important to you?

What does this success mean to you?

What benefits does this success bring?

How do you feel about your business and the work you are doing?

What is it about not having this success now that is uncomfortable?

Why is it essential that you achieve this?

What does your life look like when you have achieved it?

What will your life look like if you don't?

How will it impact on your family or friends when you achieve it?

How will they suffer if you don't?

Why are the qualities you have so important to you?

Why are the things people say about you so important to you?

List the words you have used here:

1. _____

2. _____

3. _____

4. _____

5. _____

6. _____

7. _____

8. _____

9. _____

10. _____

11. _____

12. _____

Now, look at the list and put a star next to 5 or 6 that are super-important to you and once you've done that, rank the starred ones in order of importance: 1, 2, 3, etc. This will give you your top five values – the ones that really drive you.

You may find that you learn nothing new about yourself, or, you may be really surprised to see what's really important when it comes right down to it. These words may not seem relevant to your business on first glance, but trust me, they are. They determine your purpose and, combined with your intent, they form the basis of an attractive vision that will really work for you – one that motivates you to take action!

Values

Acceptance	Effectiveness	Humility	Quality
Accomplishment	Elegance	Imagination	Relationships
Accountability	Empathy	Kindness	Relaxation
Achievement	Encouragement	Knowledge	Reliability
Adventure	Energy	Laughter	Resourcefulness
Alignment	Enlightenment	Leadership	Respect
Amusement	Entertainment	Learning	Responsibility
Assistance	Environment	Loyalty	Responsiveness
Attractiveness	Equality	Improvement	Risk
Authenticity	Ethics	Independence	Safety
Awareness	Excellence	Influence	Security
Beauty	Experience	Information	Self-awareness
Balance	Explain	Inner peace	Self-worth
Charity	Exquisiteness	Innovation	Service
Collaboration	Facilitation	Inspiration	Simplicity
Community	Fairness	Integrity	Spirituality
Connection	Faith	Intelligence	Stability
Consciousness	Fame	Joy	Stimulation
Consideration	Family	Justice	Strength
Constancy	Feeling good	Order	Success
Contentment	Fitness	Organisation	Superiority
Contribution	Freedom	Originality	Support
Cooperation	Friendship	Peace	Teaching
Courage	Fun	Peacefulness	Tenderness
Create	Generosity	Perception	Tranquillity
Creativity	Grace	Personal Dvlpmnt	Trust
Delight	Gratitude	Pleasure	Truth
Dependability	Guidance	Positive Attitude	Understanding
Dignity	Happiness	Power	Victory
Directness	Harmony	Preparation	Vision
Discovery	Health	Presence	Wealth
Diversity	Honesty	Proficiency	Wholeness
Education	Hope	Recognition	Winning

YOUR VISION

ACTIVITY 2:
CREATE YOUR TANGIBLE VISION

Create your tangible vision so that it becomes actionable and directs your subconscious mind and behaviour to that which is conducive to achieving it.

There are two options for creating your tangible vision, so choose the one that suits your preference (or do both!).

VISION BOARD

Preparation

o First, decide whether you are going to do a computerised version or a scissors and glue version. If you decide on scissors and glue, you will need a large piece of board to stick your images to.

o Make sure you won't be disturbed – you'll do a better job if you commit the time.

o Make sure you have worksheets 1 and 2 to hand – you will need this detail to create your Vision Board.

1. Gather lots of images that you feel represent the things you listed as wants or values, as well as images of anything that simply makes you feel good. If you're tearing these images from magazines, create a pile of them and if you're using the internet, collate them in a document. Try not to analyse what you are doing too much, just gather anything that stands out to you – you are going to select the best ones afterwards.

2. Sort through the images and reflect on each one for a few seconds or minutes. Choose the ones you like the most and feel you want to use.

3. Find a picture of you that represents you in a positive frame of mind, or at a positive time of your life, or a picture of your business logo if that feels like it's a better focus for the vision board. Put the picture of you or your business logo (or both) in the centre of the board.

4. Lay the other images on your board, or position them on your computer screen. As you do this, you will get a feel for how you want them to be positioned. You may choose to lay them out according to what they represent: buildings, possessions, holidays, awards, feelings, etc, or according to wants and values. Paste the images onto the board if you're using scissors and glue.

Your Vision Board is designed to inspire you every day. Your attention is incredibly powerful, so it's important that you hang it somewhere where you will see it daily. By having it visible, you will be motivated to do the things necessary to realise it.

PROVOCATIVE PROPOSITION

Preparation

- o Make sure you won't be disturbed (turn off your phone!).

- o Make sure you have worksheets 1 and 2 to hand – you will need this detail to create your Provocative Proposition.

Now, allow yourself to imagine a specific day at least 12 months in the future when your life and business is exactly as you want it to be (based on your vision).

Now, write your account of that day as if you were writing it at the end of the day. Rather than simply walking yourself through it, it is important that you immerse yourself fully in it, describing it in full detail, so that if someone else were to read it, they would also experience it as if it were them.

Start with 'Today is [day], the [date], and I...'

Describe waking up:

Where are you?
What are your surroundings? What can you see, hear, taste and touch?
How do you feel?

Describe getting ready for your day:

What do you have for breakfast?
What does it taste like?
What do you dress in?
How do you look?
How do you feel?
Why?

Describe getting on with your day:

What do you do?
Where do you go?
Who do you see?
Who do you talk to?
What about?
What do they say?
How does it make you feel?
Why?

You get the picture!

Your Provocative Proposition is designed to evoke all your senses so that the day in the future that you have created is fully experienced as if it were real. As a result, it becomes real in your subconscious mind, and as you now know, that means it's real!

Your attention is incredibly powerful, so it's important that you do not simply put your Provocative Proposition in a drawer, never to be seen again. Read it occasionally and fully immerse yourself in it when you do, as by doing so you will be motivated to do the things necessary to make it happen.

YOUR MIND-SET

ACTIVITY 3: ENSURE THAT YOUR BELIEFS, THOUGHTS AND FEELINGS ARE *ATTRACTIVE*

Ensure that your beliefs, thoughts and feelings are attractive so that they support your vision and drive your behaviour to that which is conducive to achieving it.

Remember, your success is influenced greatly by the mind-set you hold. What you believe, what you think and how you feel, dictates how you perceive and respond to situations. Like attracts like, and so your beliefs, thoughts and feelings determine the reality you experience.

This ACTivity requires you to tune into your self-talk to identify the beliefs you have that are not *attractive* and to replace them with *attractive* ones.

So, for example: if your self-talk is "If I speak in front of all those people, I'll make a fool of myself", then the belief might be: "I am no good at public speaking". If speaking publicly is an important part of your vision, then it would make sense to create an affirmative belief along the lines of "I am a coherent and confident speaker who inspires my audience". This activity will show you how. It works best when you follow the steps, including the preparation.

Preparation

- o Look at your Vision Board, or read your Provocative Proposition.

- o Notice as you pay attention to the detail of that vision what your self-talk is like.

- o Try not to attach to the thoughts, just notice them.

- o Be aware of the potential of more negative thinking becoming evident as a result of becoming more aware of your negative thinking and remember this: if you think you can change your beliefs, then you can!

WORKSHEET 3   YOUR MIND-SET – SELF-TALK

The things I say to myself often

What you write down here is hugely important as it highlights the specific self-talk you need to address in order to change the belief responsible.

The new beliefs I have

Now, ask yourself this question: "What beliefs will attract the people, opportunities and things to me that will make this vision a reality?" It is helpful at this stage to revisit the things you wrote above, as the self-talk you highlighted is likely to indicate which thoughts need changing as a priority.

Write down the beliefs that you want to have. Remember that intent is stronger than conditioning, and 'want' is stronger than 'need', so really focus on what you want to believe about yourself and your business.

The new thoughts I have

Now that you have a list of desired beliefs, ask yourself this question: "What thoughts do I need to have in order to make those beliefs a reality?" Remember that thoughts become things, so ask yourself: "What thoughts will attract the things I want?" and be sure to frame them in positive language.

The feelings I want to feel

Now ask yourself this question: "Through this vision, what feelings am I aiming to generate?" Remember, everything you do is with the intention of generating a feeling, and whilst your feelings are linked to your thoughts, you can also influence how you feel directly by doing the stuff that you know will generate the feelings you want.

The activities I want to do more of

Now ask yourself this question: "What can I do now to feel this way?" and then for each feeling, write down the activities that if you did them would make you feel that way. For example: working on specific types of projects, doing specific activities, working with specific people, celebrating in a specific type of way, etc. If this is challenging, recall a time in the past when you felt this way and then write down what the circumstances were. What were you doing? Who was around you?

My affirmation

- o With your vision and your new beliefs, thoughts and feelings in mind, write a statement of a couple of short sentences which is framed in positive language and describes the essence of where and who you want to be.

- o Phrase the statement as if it were true now. So, for instance: "I am making progress every day" is preferable to "I want to make progress every day". Remember, you are not trying to 'want' something. You are trying to make it reality.

- o Place your affirmation where it is constantly visible (on the mirror you use daily, by the kettle, in your car, on your computer screen). Make sure that you are confronted with it daily as a minimum, hourly where possible and ideally constantly!

- o Every time you see it, say it to yourself intentionally, both silently and out loud.

- o Share your affirmation with other people.

- o Record yourself saying it and play it back to yourself, or write it down when you're doodling, repeat it to yourself over and over – sing it if you want to!

After a period of between 21 days and three months of consistent conscious effort, you can embed this statement as part of your mind-set.

YOUR MIND-SET

ACTIVITY 4:
CREATE UNQUESTIONABLE EVIDENCE

Create unquestionable evidence so that your mind is conditioned to believe you are both capable and credible.

Remember, when someone else's credibility is in question, we tend to look for evidence of their work to convince ourselves that they can do the job. The same approach works in conditioning our own mind about our own credibility, so this activity is about bringing into your conscious awareness real evidence of your own capability and credibility.

Preparation

o Spend some time reflecting on your life and recalling your successes. A 'success' is defined as something that you did well and that gave you satisfaction. It does not need to be extraordinary, it just has to have involved you doing something well. Your 'successes' reflect your entire life from birth to date. They relate to every area of your life: school, work, leisure, friendships, family and intimate relationships.

o You may choose to recall highlights from your life, but what's most important for this activity is what you actually **did**.

o Try not to analyse or evaluate your successes. No matter how insignificant you may feel it might appear to someone else, if it gave *you* satisfaction (not your friends and family – *you*!) at the time then it is a success. This is not the time to be modest – there is no value in modesty here.

WORKSHEET 4   YOUR MIND-SET – EVIDENCE

Your successes

Write down as many successes as you can recall here. What you write down here is hugely important as it brings into conscious awareness your skills and strengths to convince your own mind of your capability and credibility.

Now, reflect on the successes you have recalled and select two to write about in more detail. Ideally, the two you choose will be the two that made you feel the strongest.

Success 1

Age:

How I got involved.

What I did and how I did it.

What was so satisfying.

Success 2

Age:

How I got involved.

What I did and how I did it.

What was so satisfying.

Your strengths

Now that you have been through the process of recalling and reflecting on your successes, spend some time reflecting specifically on your strengths.

Remember, a 'strength' is not just something that you do well – it's something that you do well and that makes you feel stronger. A strength is something that energises you and that you could do all day long without tiring. It's the thing that others notice about you and possibly even remark on. So, what have you done in your life that has made you feel energised? What could you talk about or do for hours? What would you do even if you didn't get paid?

Write down all the things that you are good at but which also make you feel strong. If it helps, ask other people or recall compliments you've had or read testimonials that others have written about you.

_____

_____

_____

_____

_____

_____

_____

_____

_____

_____

Once you've listed your strengths, put a star next to the ones that are really relevant to your vision. Now list your relevant knowledge, skills and experience here:

The relevant knowledge I have

The relevant skills I have

The relevant experience I have

Congratulations – you now have unquestionable evidence of your capability and credibility.

ACTION

ACTION is your **external activity**. It's about both how you 'Act', in other words, the actions you take that others notice, and it's also about the intentional actions you take towards a specific outcome or goal.

ACTION is essentially how ATTRACT (your internal activity) manifests on the outside: in what you say, what you do, how you react and who you hang out with, and the perception that others have about you as a result. It is also how ATTRACT manifests in the daily activities you do to ensure that you move closer towards your vision.

What you say and do and how you say and do those things impacts significantly on what you attract.

ACTION looks at the two elements of your external activity: YOUR BEHAVIOUR and YOUR PLAN.

YOUR BEHAVIOUR

Behaviour is our response to all stimuli in conjunction with our environment, whether that's internal or external, conscious or subconscious, overt or covert, voluntary or involuntary.

Behaviour is the aspect of our activity that is visible to other people. It plays a huge part in how other people perceive who we are and what we stand for, and because perception is reality, our behaviour plays an essential role in The Act Of Attraction!

As you know, your behaviour is driven by the beliefs you hold in your subconscious mind. Once you have an *attractive* vision and *attractive* thoughts and feelings that are aligned with that vision, the appropriate behaviour will inevitably follow. However, that does not mean that you can't also become consciously aware of your current behaviour and make intentional changes now to support your *attraction*.

This means identifying which of your current behaviours are congruent with what you want to achieve and who you want to be, as well as those that aren't, and then consciously making changes to your behaviour so that it becomes *attractive.*

This may appear contrived at first. I have had clients ask me: "Isn't it better to just be yourself?" Absolutely. If 'being' is 'behaving' and 'yourself' is 'the person you are when you are approaching your life and business with clarity of intent and purpose and with thoughts, feelings and behaviours that back that up', then that's exactly what this section is about.

Being 'yourself' is the ultimate in being authentic, and authenticity is an important aspect of living genuine success. However, being 'yourself' does not always work in the pursuit of success for all people. For some, simply being who they are right now means behaving unconsciously and on autopilot, acting out old conditioning without being aware of it, to the extent that it negatively affects what they attract in their lives and, in effect, their wellbeing. That's not desirable surely? And, it's certainly not *attractive.*

When I talk about aligning your behaviour with your vision, I am not advocating being someone else, or acting in a way that is not authentic.

This is not about putting on an act.

Being you is clearly preferable to trying to be someone else. However, the reality is that our conditioning and the auto-response nature of the mind/behaviour connection often leads to us exhibiting behaviour that does not truly reflect who we are or what we stand for.

What I **am** encouraging you to do is to consciously develop behaviour that represents your intent ('what' you want) and your purpose ('why' you want it) because when your behaviour represents those things, it represents who you **really** are.

'Being yourself' is good advice when it involves deciding who you want to be and how you want to be perceived by others, and then behaving in a way that is congruent with that. Then you truly ARE being yourself – you are being the 'yourself' that you choose to be. You are being the best you that you can be and when you are being the best YOU that you can be, you begin to operate from a point of self-approval which impacts your self-esteem positively. And in addition, you receive approval from the people that share the same values as you do. And that is *attractive*.

Creating your *attractive* Behaviour

In addition to the personal benefits of behaving in a way that is congruent with your vision, there are other benefits too. All successful people recognise that their success comes through and as a result of other people – other people are absolutely key to our success. People follow us, support us, advocate for us and they also buy from us. Whatever it is you want to achieve, you need other people in order to do it.

So, there is no getting away from it – if we want to attract the things we want into our lives, other people's perception of us is important.

The way other people perceive our behaviour is not always apparent (unless of course they tell us), and mostly, we become aware of what others think and say about what we say and do when it shows up in our *Reputation*.

REPUTATION

Reputation is the estimation or opinion in which others commonly hold a person, a company or a product. We are who we are, based on our values, beliefs and behaviours and those things define our character. Our reputation is driven by other people's **perception** of who we are, and it is not the by-product of what we say and do, but the by-product of what others think and say about what we say and do. Character is what's on the inside whereas reputation is what's on the outside.

Whether we like it or not, we are being evaluated every day by our peers, our clients and our friends – both as individuals and based on our associations with other people and groups. This evaluation is being made, based not entirely on who we are, but on who we lead people to believe we are, based on the behaviour that we demonstrate repeatedly over time.

I read somewhere once that character is more important than reputation. The implication is that we should be more concerned with our character than with our reputation, as character is what we **really** are, whereas reputation is what others think about us. On the surface, this makes sense. I worked with someone once who was so concerned with managing his reputation that when his real character was revealed, he lost a large client. He didn't do anything particularly unethical, or behave wildly different to how many people behave, but because what he said and did was so in conflict with his carefully managed reputation, the trust broke down. The irony is that had he been less focused on managing his reputation based on what he thought it 'should' be, and instead allowed his real character to come through, he may not have been perceived as such a let-down.

If character is so important, and reputation is how character manifests in our behaviour and what other people think and say about us as a result, then surely reputation is equally as important as character? Think about it: You might have a sound character based on sound intent and values, but if other people perceive your behaviour to demonstrate values that are different to your real values, how is that helpful? It's certainly not *attractive.*

I worked with someone who was completely unconcerned about his reputation. Whilst he claimed to be all about helping people, much of his behaviour was in conflict with that. If he perceived that he was being challenged or threatened, the behaviour he exhibited was often aggressive and offensive. As a result, he developed a reputation for being a bully which, whilst understandable, was not necessarily entirely accurate. So, you can see that character and reputation are intertwined, and in the context of *attraction*, they are both equally as important as each other.

It is not enough to simply **be** the person that you want to be, you need to also be **seen** to be that person too.

I have observed interactions between people where one walks away with an impression of the other which I have felt is inaccurate based on my own experience of that person. Yet, I can see why that impression was made. And I have observed behaviour from some people that conflicts with what they claim to be about. So, why does this happen? Often when people feel inadequate or threatened, their behaviour reflects those feelings rather than their values. Whilst this reaction may be perfectly natural (it's the autopilot process in action that I mentioned earlier), the perception it creates can have a damaging effect on their reputation if other people are vocal about the impression it leaves.

When our reputation is *attractive*, it can result in admiration and following and it can open doors. When it's not *attractive*, it can close doors.

Ultimately, perception is reality and so very often reputation *precedes* reality – it precedes **us**. If you look around you now at your wider network, there will be some people with whom you identify based mainly or even solely on their reputation. You will have positive impressions of some of them and you might even feel comfortable recommending them to others, even though you have never worked with them or met them personally. If you removed reputation from the equation, many of those people would simply be strangers with whom you have little way of relating.

Reputation is a great time-saver as it means that we don't have to develop relationships with each and every person, company or product in order to make a judgement. However, the same also applies with regards to us.

You may not care what people think of you, but do you care what they say? People make judgements about us not just on what they see but also on what they hear, and so if you are not ensuring that your reputation is in line with your vision, then you are literally leaving it up to others to decide what it is and whether or not you achieve it.

You may already know that you have a good reputation. You might have created it by accident, or you might have decided what you wanted to be known for and created that reputation consciously. You may already know that you do not have the reputation you want, or you may not be aware of what your reputation is. Whatever the case, one thing is absolutely certain: you DO have one and it is already showing up in your business.

ACTivity 5 in The ACT Of ACTION section on page 147 will guide you through identifying your reputation.

Creating your *attractive* Reputation

An *attractive* reputation is one that is based on your vision (it is intentional and purposeful), which shows in the behaviour that other people observe. An *attractive* reputation is one that attracts desired people, circumstances and opportunities to you. An *attractive* reputation is one that is consistent regardless of the social group (work, social, family, etc). An *attractive* reputation is one that starts from inside and is based on the most fundamental aspect of *attraction* there is: INTEGRITY.

Many people think of integrity as being about honesty and adherence to moral and ethical principles. Actually, integrity is more complex than that. Integrity is the condition of 'wholeness', where our language and behaviour are consistent with the type of person we present ourselves to be. Some say that integrity is what you do when no-one is watching.

When you think about it, the whole Act of Attraction piece is about integrity, because it's about the state of wholeness, and it's through aligning one's internal and external activity that wholeness is achieved.

Integrity is formed through repeated, consistent behaviour over time and it plays an integral part in personal wellbeing. As you know, our personal values and beliefs define who we are and they drive our thoughts, our feelings and our behaviour. They also influence our decisions, our reactions and our self-image. When our own behaviour is in line with our beliefs and values, we feel good about ourselves, and when it isn't, we feel the opposite.

So, why do we sometimes act in ways that are not congruent with our beliefs or values?

There are lots of reasons for this and I am sure you'll relate to one if not all of them. Sometimes we find ourselves in situations where due to fear, or uncertainty, or due to other people's expectations or a sense of obligation, we compromise our values. Sometimes we are not consciously aware that we are doing it and sometimes we are aware and we find ourselves doing it anyway. If we continue to behave in ways that conflict with our internal values, eventually we become aware of a strong feeling of internal conflict which, if left alone, can impact our self-image and create physiological symptoms, like anxiety and stress.

Of course, there are exceptions to this. There are times when we are not operating in line with our values, where we are also not in conflict. For instance, you may not normally be comfortable shouting at people, or telling people what to do, but if a fire starts in a bucket next to someone, you might find that your values go out of the window in favour of keeping them safe. Personally, I'd welcome this reaction in you if the bucket was next to me!

However, when there is internal conflict, it is known as cognitive dissonance. Cognitive dissonance is the feeling of discomfort that arises when we experience conflicting thoughts, beliefs, values or emotional reactions simultaneously. The discomfort is experienced literally like a tension between two or more feelings or thoughts and it is experienced most powerfully when it is related to our own self-image. It is also the psychological discomfort caused by failing to act as we think we should. So, in simple terms, if we believe that we are fundamentally good and then do something that we perceive as being bad, the discomfort we feel as a result is cognitive dissonance. If you recall a time now when you felt foolish or embarrassed – that was dissonance in action.

Even if the conflict between our behaviour and our values and beliefs is due to feeling compelled by circumstances beyond our control or feeling that we have no choice, this internal conflict is still the result.

So, what can we do about it?

Sometimes the desire to relieve the conflict will lead to us changing one or other of the conflicting beliefs or actions. So, we change our actions to relieve the tension, or we justify our actions by changing the conflicting cognition. Sometimes if our actions cannot be undone, the conflict can feel so uncomfortable that it can compel us to change our beliefs to ones that fit with the behaviour. Sound familiar?

Remember that time when you felt strongly about something that someone did, or said, yet when confronted with the opportunity to voice how you felt, you didn't. Perhaps it was for fear of the consequences or simply to keep the peace. The problem is though, that you ended up going along with something that fundamentally conflicted with your own values and so you felt resentful towards them, or disappointed or even angry with yourself.

I've been there a number of times. I worked with the HR department of a large investment bank where the company culture 'talked about' their commitment to work/life balance and yet the energy within the HR department itself was in complete conflict with that. The staff worked 12-hour days (even though the department was over-staffed), because the actual culture on the ground was one of 'face-time' where people felt they needed to be seen at their desks to show their commitment. This is just one example of many. Initially, I sought to influence the culture, but after a while I found myself behaving like everyone else. I'd get to work at 8am and I'd remain at my desk until 8pm, pretending to be 'working'.

I began to feel increasingly like I was compromising on what I believed was important. I began to feel resentful towards the company and disappointed in myself and it had a significant effect on my own wellbeing, not simply because of the energy I was expending, but also because of the impact it had on my own sense of integrity.

The existence of cognitive dissonance confirms that integrity is not just a desirable trait, but an integral part of our psychological wellbeing which is why for me the whole integrity piece is so important.

This internal conflict is not only experienced in relation to our own behaviour, but it also occurs when we observe inconsistencies between what someone else claims to be about and how they actually behave – whether we do it consciously or subconsciously, we question their integrity. If you have ever had that feeling that you didn't trust someone but were unable to put your finger on why, that's cognitive dissonance occurring at a subconscious level. It means that on an intuitive level you have observed an inconsistency between their vocal and actual behaviour.

Again, I have experienced this in a huge way. In another role, when I perceived the decisions and actions of people I worked with to be in conflict with the culture we had created and cited publicly, I couldn't help but voice it, and whilst it created conflict and disharmony externally, internally I had my integrity intact. Later as it became clear that my power to influence things was diminishing, it was the commitment I'd made and a strong sense of obligation that resulted in me subconsciously seeking to change my internal beliefs and values to 'live with it'. Because my counter-values were so strong, living with it resulted in me waking up daily with horrendous internal conflict which I experienced like a tug-o-war between what my head (logic and investment), my heart (loyalty and commitment) and my gut (intuition) were telling me.

Fortunately, I had the foresight and psychological grounding to recognise what was happening internally and so I changed my behaviour. It meant letting go and walking away from something that I'd invested a lot in, and that meant a huge amount to me, which was very painful, but it also meant retaining my integrity and wellbeing – without which, for me, the rest was meaningless.

This type of internal conflict is often experienced as a 'gut feeling' and in my experience, it should never be ignored.

Who have you known who has talked about the importance of empowering others and then acted like a control freak? Who have you worked with who has claimed to be results focused and then failed to deliver? Who have you known who has claimed to not abide rudeness and then abused the waiter whilst you were out at dinner? It is entirely possible that the things these people claimed were important to them really were. But, because their behaviour was not aligned with that, regardless of what they may have believed, thought and said, unless you knew them well, you probably judged them based on what they actually did. It's true that actions often speak louder than words.

In the same way that cognitive dissonance occurs in us when other people's behaviour conflicts with their portrayed image, it also occurs in other people when they perceive what **we** say and do to be conflicted. Cognitive dissonance is not *attractive*, so we should be doing everything we can to avoid experiencing it ourselves, and generating it in others.

What is *attractive* is behaviour that is aligned with your vision and a reputation that is congruent with your character. And this is where *Leadership* plays an important role.

LEADERSHIP

There are many definitions of leadership out there, but the consistent theme through all of them is 'influence'. In the context of The Act Of Attraction, leadership is the process of social influence in which we enlist the support of others in the accomplishment of our vision.

I used to speak a lot on leadership to business audiences and when I asked people to put their hands up if they were a leader, many of them did not. This interests me because it suggests that many people still see leadership as being about authority as opposed to influence. Whether you are a parent, a teacher, a trainer or a business person, your success is dependent on your ability to influence others to follow you. This makes you a leader.

Throughout my career, I have worked with dozens of leaders, and most recently I was involved in placing many business owners in leadership positions and developing those leaders to do the same. Many of these people had been managers in previous jobs and many had not held a leadership role prior. Sometimes they did not see themselves as leaders and were surprised when I approached them. The truth is that often, my reasons for offering them a leadership role had little to do with their business or leadership experience. It also rarely had much to do with their skills. It was almost always about their behaviour and how that showed up in their reputation and their ability to influence others.

You see, people are influenced more by the way we **behave** than they are influenced by the things we can do. Behaviour is *attractive*. It draws people to us who are of a like mind or have similar values. Skills are about doing, whereas behaviour is about being. Some people argue that skills can be learned and behaviour is innate. That implies that behaviour cannot be learned. I disagree. All behaviour is learned and our behaviour changes over time. Just like we can change our beliefs, we can also change our behaviour, if we choose to.

Remember, success comes through and as a result of other people. What they think and feel about you comes through how they perceive what you say and how you act. So if you want to achieve something, then how you influence people and situations is key, and you do that through your behaviour.

Remember, you want to attract the things into your life that you **want**, which means behaving in a way that is in line with that. I am not suggesting that you become overly conscious or robotic or that you try to be something you are not – that is the opposite of *attractive*. What I am suggesting is that you become mindful of your own behaviour and how that is perceived by others so that you behave in a way that is in line with your vision. That way you positively influence your *attraction*.

In a business context, you do this through the 4 LEAD channels:

Language
Educate
Attitude
Demonstrate

L is for **Language**

We've covered the importance of language in YOUR VISION and YOUR MIND-SET.

Language in this context is about the words we use. Whether verbally, in person or on the phone, in writing by email or letter, or through blogging or on social media, the language we use contributes to the perception people have about who we are and what we stand for.

You may have heard the saying 'communication is the response you get'. What this means is that if you do not get the response you intended, you failed to communicate effectively. If you think about it, this is a principle that can be applied in *attraction* full stop – you receive the response you want when you communicate what you want clearly. The words you use are key to this.

When you seek to communicate a message or to influence another person, the language you use is extremely important. Each word you use contains meaning from which other people gain understanding and because people think in words and sentences, when you are able to influence language, you effectively influence thought.

The words you use affect the impact you have through your verbal communication.

Here's an example: I want to work with highly skilled and somewhat already successful business owners who have goals and the passion and drive to achieve them but who lack the know-how or resources to do so. This is because, working with people who fit this profile makes me feel energised and satisfies my desire and need for results. So, when I am out and about talking to people about my business, I make sure that I say exactly that. I use those exact words. I don't just say that I work with small business owners, as the danger there is that the referrals I receive might include business owners who don't fit my ideal client profile. I **lead** my network through my language to refer me my ideal client. And they do.

Here's another example. In a previous role where I led a team of leaders to lead and manage the team who ran fortnightly business breakfast meetings, I was very clear about some of the language we used. It was important that our leaders felt part of a bigger team and so we had developed a culture of collaboration and teamwork. We strongly advocated 'doing your bit' towards the vision and that collective effort was important. Everyone had a valuable role to play in the bigger picture. Many of our team members had come from previous employment and for them the decision to work for themselves was borne out of a desire to have the flexibility and freedom that they didn't feel they had when they had a 'job'. For these reasons, we explicitly used the words 'collectively supporting' as part of our documented culture and the word 'role' to describe each leadership position.

I could provide many examples of this, but I think you get the point? Words have meaning for people and so it is worth spending a little bit of time thinking about the words you use in your business and asking yourself if they are in line with your intent and purpose.

E is for **EDUCATE**

Education is the act or the process of imparting information and messages.

In this context it's about our knowledge and our experience and how that culminates in our reputation. It's about both the information and the messages we put out into the market place (in other words, our marketing) or our social network and how we use that to engage with our audience and to create client *attraction.*

Education that is *attractive* is information that is in line with your intent and purpose. Remember, communication is the response you get, and so attracting what you want is reliant on communicating appropriate information and messages. Language plays an important part in this as does content, but it's also about the method you use. Whether it's books, blogs, seminars, videos or other media, your method says almost as much about who you are and what you stand for as your content.

For instance, if your business is involved with training, then you might favour recording a video showing you delivering training as well as blogging about the topic you train people on. If part of your business or personal brand is related to social media, it makes sense to consciously use the various social media channels to transmit your education. If you are a personal trainer, then using lots of social media channels is less important from an integrity perspective. People are more likely to associate you with being active and outdoors, so video blogging outdoors might work better for you. However, if you are a personal trainer who works predominantly with young people, then using social media to engage with them is arguably more effective than sending leaflets through the mail.

Do you want to be an expert?

Educate is also about our expert or authority status. Think about someone you know who is not just an expert, but who is **known** to be an expert. When they put something out into the market place, people tend to pay attention, don't they? That's because people who are considered an authority in their field command respect. They also often command higher fees.

In business, there is a strong connection between our level of perceived expertise and our financial income. This is an important point. If you've worked in different roles, then it's likely that you have lots of different skills. You can probably do lots of things well. Many of us fall into this 'generalist' camp, and whilst this gives us a rounded skill-set and enables us to add significant value, from an education perspective it's not *attractive.* Think about it. The more general your messaging is, the more ambiguous it is and the more difficult it is therefore for people to relate and attach to it. So, whilst you may have a rounded skill-set, your messaging is more *attractive* if it's aligned with the specific outcome you want to achieve. When you are pointed with your messaging, you increase your *attraction* significantly.

Pointing your messages

Having worked within the business networking world for over five years, I have witnessed many different approaches to education in terms of messaging. The biggest mistake that most people make is to tell people about what they do and how they do it, rather than tell people about the results they deliver and why. Again, we're back to 'intent' and 'purpose'. In this context, intent describes the 'what', not in terms of what you do to deliver a result, but 'what' in terms of the actual **result** you deliver, and purpose describes the 'why' as in the 'reason' you deliver that result.

Taking the first point – intent ('what'): people are rarely interested in **what** you **do**, what they are interested in is what you can do **for them**. I learned this the hard way. In the first six months I was in business, I used to stand up at networking events and say "My name is Tamsen Garrie and I am a Clinical Hypnotherapist!". I would then describe the process I used and the issues I dealt with.

It took me a while to work out that people were not tuned in to what I was saying and it took me a little longer to work out why: I was not tuning in to them! Rather than seeking to have them understand what solution I offered to the problems they experienced, I was seeking to educate them about my profession and me.

Once I worked this out, I started to focus my messaging on **results** and the impact was quite phenomenal. Whilst many people continued to have no real understanding of how I did what I did, they did begin to believe that through working with me, they could eradicate negative beliefs, thoughts, feelings and behaviours and develop more positive and productive ones – ones that were *attractive*. My practice grew very fast as I developed a reputation for a no-nonsense, results-focused approach to shifting people's mind-sets and enabling them to create successful outcomes. And, it wasn't long before I had a full practice.

Taking the second point – purpose ('why'): people relate more to 'why' you do what you do than they relate to 'how' you do what you do. The more evident your personal motivation is, the more attractive your messaging will be. I'll touch more on this later when we talk about stories.

Having grown that business and having been involved at director level developing and leading a national business network, I currently run a 'business and people development business', working with other business owners to develop the vision, mind-set and plan of action to grow their business. Having learned the importance of education in the context of leadership, I am now very clear in my messaging about the types of people I work with: 'highly skilled and somewhat already successful business owners who have goals and the passion and drive to achieve them but who lack the know-how or resources to do so'.

I spent a fair amount of time working that ideal client profile out, so that when I did start educating my market, I knew exactly what my message was and who I was pointing my message at, and why. I've developed a process and a product specifically for that type of client and I have a fee structure that appeals to that type of client too. My social media activity is a combination of **engagement** (interacting with my business friends and associates) and **transmission** (links to my own blogs and information put out by others in the areas that are relevant to my market and my business). Whilst I am 'myself' in my interactions through social media, I am always mindful of what I want to achieve and of not sending messages out that conflict with that.

Your version of 'educate' depends on your 'what' and your 'why' and what those things mean you want to attract. If your outcome involves influencing change, then what you put out there in the market place plays a key part. You need to know what it is that you're about and then you need to tell people. Most people will not take the time to try and work out what you stand for and the value you bring. So, if you don't tell them, they will never know. This means having the courage to do a little self-promotion.

Self-promotion

Self-promotion is not everyone's cup of tea. To be honest, it's not really mine. I am personally irritated by excessive public self-adoration. I find it icky (technical term!) and unattractive. However, this is not about judgement. I don't have an opinion about whether it's right or wrong, I just have a preference. In fact, I believe that we Brits can err a little too much on the 'modesty' side and that many people could benefit from being a bit bolder in their promotion of themselves and their offerings.

The way I prefer to **receive** promotional messages is through a combination of self-promotion and promotion via other sources. For me, this feels more real, because it is based on other people's experience and perception and not just that of the person in question. It also demonstrates confidence both in the person himself or herself and in those they have worked with. Because this is how I prefer to receive that education, I choose to apply that combination in my own messaging.

Whatever education you put out in the market place will attract a response and it is not for me to advise you either way. The only thing I would say is this: whilst confident people who stand by their messages instil confidence in their market, and that is *attractive*, what isn't *attractive* is self-promotion without substance. If you're going to say you're good, then please, please be good. Remember, the louder and more visible you are, the more attention you'll attract and so be clear that if what you attract is not in keeping with your vision, the level to which you attract it will be greater the louder you shout!

Facts tell, stories sell

Whilst statistics and facts are interesting for some, they mostly engage the left brain. Stories on the other hand engage the right brain because they capture people on an emotional level, creating a deeper connection. Stories feel more real than facts because people can relate personally to them – this also makes them more memorable.

Remember, education in the context of leadership is about influencing other people. If you want to create a shift in thinking, or a change in behaviour, then a powerful way to do that is to use story telling.

You'll notice that I have used stories in this book. It's intentional. Stories are powerful because they provide context as well as information and because they evoke emotion in others. I saw a beautiful example of this last month.

At a women's networking event that I run in my local town, a member was presenting her 'member slot', a ten minute speaking slot where a member shares information about their business with the rest of the group. This lady works for a solicitors' firm based around the South West of England and she specialises in accident compensation law. Now, correct me if I am wrong, but I suspect that unless you've ever been in need of an accident lawyer, or have a friend or family member who has, OR you are one yourself, then this subject does not excite you? If it does, that's okay too!

She told us a true story. A man in his 20s had died in a car accident, leaving a wife and two children. At the hearing, this solicitor who was working in another area of law at the time had asked the wife if there was anything she could do to further support her. The wife had broken down, explaining that she had no job and two children to look after and no idea how she was going to keep her home going. This solicitor worked on her claim and managed to secure a significant compensation deal that meant she could keep her home and continue to provide for her children. It was the work that this solicitor did for this lady and the impact it had on her life and her children that led to her making the decision to specialise in this type of law. The decision was not driven by financial goals, or even because of an interest in the law itself, it was made because of the personal satisfaction she felt at the impact of her work on this lady's life and the huge sense of purpose she felt as a result.

The room was transfixed as she told this story and whilst none of us are, even now, possibly any the wiser on the ins and outs of accident law (I'm probably not even using the right term for it!), we all understand now the result she delivers. More importantly for her, not one of us will struggle to identify her ideal client should we ever come across them – *attractive* education.

There is nothing more compelling than a well-told story. Stories can demonstrate a point more than simply sharing the facts. They can make a person seem more real so that people can relate to them. Stories are *attractive.*

I learned the power of story telling when I studied hypnosis and I used it a lot in the early days of developing my practice. My discovery of hypnosis as a powerful tool to help me at a challenging time in my own life was far more compelling than sharing the theory and science behind hypnosis.

This doesn't mean that you have to turn every single blog or talk into a personal, life-changing story, it just means thinking about how you can inject the human element into your message so that it engages people on a personal and emotional level.

A is for **Attitude**

Attitude is essentially about the 'purpose' aspect of vision and it's the entire mind-set piece. It's our personal values, our belief systems and what we think and feel. It's also about our self-image, which combines our self-esteem and self-efficacy. And, it's about how all these things are exhibited through our behaviour.

Attitude is also about how we react to things – especially when things go wrong. It's about how we deal with self-doubt and fear and how we respond to failure and rejection.

I was working with a client whose team do a fair amount of cold calling to get new clients. We were working on their conversation strategy for the calls and one of his team told me that she found it difficult not to take rejection personally. Another colleague told her not to take it personally, that rejection was 'just part of the job'. My take on it was this: it's not easy to see rejection as anything other than personal. The word 'rejection' literally means to be 'cast away', or 'discarded' (remember the power of language). The need for 'acceptance' is a basic human need and so it would be almost abnormal not to feel bad about being discarded.

I suggested she change her 'attitude' towards what she was currently viewing as rejection. In other words, rather than seeking to change what was actually a perfectly acceptable response to the situation, I asked her to change her **perception** of the situation itself. I asked her what other reason there could be for someone not wanting to talk to her on the phone. We listed all the reasons we could think of, none of which related to her personally in any way. And so I asked the question: "Do these reasons represent rejection?" Of course they didn't. As a result a whole new attitude was adopted by the entire team – one that enabled them to get on with the job at hand. Within a few weeks, their conversion rate from suspect to prospect had doubled – literally.

When you are able to change your attitude to something, the emotional reaction you have is different. Can you see how powerful attitude is?

Our attitude is also reflected in the way we view and therefore treat other people and it can draw them to us, or it can repel them from us. So for instance, if we are genuinely interested in others, it shows through our attitude: we ask questions and more importantly we listen to the responses. We appear attentive and we respond appropriately to questions asked of us.

How many times have you been in a networking situation and the other person is looking over your shoulder at the door, or around the room? It may not reflect their entire attitude, but what it says to you in that moment is: they're just not that interested. I have to keep a check on this myself as I can have a tendency to be attached to my mobile phone, and so when I am meeting someone for coffee, unless I am awaiting an important call or email, I put it away in my bag. That's because I **am** genuinely interested in them and so, equally, I want them to **see** that I am.

It's not for me (or anyone) to tell you what attitude you should have, that's up to you. What I am advising is that you ensure that your attitude supports your vision and that it is reflected in your behaviour, whether that's when interacting directly with people, or through your education.

D is for **Demonstrate**

This is arguably the most important part of leadership as it pulls the rest together.

Demonstrate is about how our language, education and attitude manifest in our behaviour and how that convinces other people of what we're about. It's about living in our integrity: being authentic, behaving in a way that is congruent with what we claim to be, living our press and walking our talk. It's the stuff that other people observe and remark on and how that inspires their own behaviour.

Ultimately, the demonstration aspect of LEAD is about the demonstration of your beliefs and values through your behaviour. This means **being** who you say you are so that you are not only that person, but that you are also **seen** to be that person. This is *attractive.*

Attractive demonstration is behaviour that creates the magnetic draw that I talked about at the start of the book, so that you attract to you the people, circumstances and opportunities you want. This is evident in the way you appear, how you live your life and how you approach and respond to other people.

A big part of this is our physical appearance. This isn't just about how we look though, it's about how we **appear** to others. It is how we look and dress, but it's also how we present ourselves physically, like how we stand and walk and the body language we exhibit while we're doing those things. We've all been in that situation where someone has talked about one thing and their body language has conflicted with that. Confidence is a great example. I remember at a networking event, a guy stood up and introduced himself as a NLP (Neuro Linguistic Programming) practitioner. He went on to describe the work he did with individuals to create high performance. As he spoke, he stood with his hands clasped, his eyes transfixed on the table in front of him and his shoulders slumped. He looked uncomfortable and appeared to lack in that moment the very thing he claimed to be able to help others to develop. Now, this is the interesting thing. If he has the NLP skills, then he may very well have the ability to help people develop high performance. The problem though is that he failed to convince me or the people in the room of that. If he'd lifted his shoulders back and allowed his eyes to meet the eyes of those in the room, he might have been more convincing. If we want to instil confidence in others, how we present ourselves is absolutely key.

It starts with a smile. A smile is incredibly *attractive*, for two reasons. The first reason is that it makes us feel good. Did you know that it is almost impossible to feel bad when we smile? Even a forced smile makes us feel more positive. That's because the muscles we move when we turn the corners of our lips upwards apply pressure on our brain, which triggers a release of serotonin, a happy hormone that induces a feeling of wellbeing. Smiling changes your attitude in an instant. When we smile, we feel more positive and when we feel positive, we think more positively and we behave more positively – all of which are *attractive*. I remember vividly the first time I learned this simple technique and I have applied it consciously ever since. For the most part, when I smile it's because I am enjoying myself or feel good, but sometimes I force myself to smile even when I am not feeling that way. By doing so, I trick my mind into thinking more positively and as a result, I feel better. Try it!

The second reason that smiling is *attractive* is that it is it is also difficult for others not to respond to a smile with a smile (remember, like attracts like). When you meet someone for the first time and they smile warmly at you, you are drawn to them. You enjoy that person's company more and so you want to be around them. Smiling is a very simple, but very powerful aspect of *attraction*.

I advocated using this as a conscious engagement strategy when working at business and trade shows. It's common for exhibitors to give away free stuff, like chocolates, or pens, etc. Our engagement strategy was to give out free smiles. We wore 'smile' badges and we would ask the delegates as they went by "would you like a free smile?" It was very rare that someone did not stop and smile back, and more often than not, they stopped at our stand.

Live your future history now

Demonstration is also about behaving as if you already have the things you want. The great thing about appearing to be what we aspire to be now is that not only do we create that reality internally, but we *attract* that reality externally too. Do you remember the section about doing activities that create the feelings now in order to create the outcome you want? This is the same thing. When you behave like you have the things you want now, you create the relevant feelings and behaviour now!

So, if you want to be successful, act successfully. If you want to feel energetic, act energetically. This is not about pretending you are something you are not. It is like the smiling thing. If you smile, you feel good and others do too. If you stand straight and tall, you feel more confident and you instil confidence in others. If you look someone in the eye when you are talking to him or her, you imply interest and so you attract it back. And the best bit is that when you make these conscious changes, the feelings you generate are real and that is authentic. It **is** possible to be authentic and also behave in a way that depicts the person you aspire to be.

This can be taken a little further than behaviour too. I have applied this 'living your future history now' in a very tangible way over the past six years.

Back in 2006, I had just returned to the UK from Australia and I had just started my business. Money was tight and so I was renting a house and I had borrowed a friend's car – a clapped-out rusty VW Golf. I had a clear business vision back then with a specific business income and personal salary I wanted to pay myself. Realising that perception is everything and seeing the value in demonstrating success in order to achieve it, I went out and bought a car that I knew I would be able to afford in 12 months' time once I'd achieved a number of the goals within my vision. It wasn't an Audi R8, it was a Peugeot 206, but when I drove it, I felt like I knew I would feel when I achieved those goals – and that felt amazing. Instead of living in a state of 'when I...', I was living in a state of 'I am...' and so my behaviour changed to suit that. That is the power of demonstration.

Of course, I am not suggesting for one minute that you get into debt. I am simply demonstrating here through my own experience that sometimes we need to literally step into the future now, not just in terms of our mind-set, but also in terms of the things we surround ourselves with. The following year, I bought a Peugeot 307 cc and two years later my Audi TT. Each time, I bought the car that my future vision would enable me to buy. Living your future history right now has strong intent, and remember, intent is *attractive.*

Modelling *attractive* behaviour

You may have heard of modelling before. It is an NLP term that describes the process of recreating excellence through studying a specific human behaviour and mastering the psychology (beliefs and thoughts) and physiology (reactions and actions) that underlie that behaviour. It is the process of achieving an outcome by studying how someone else has gone about achieving the same outcome and then applying the same behaviour. Modelling is a complex subject and I only want to talk about it here in the context of demonstration (i.e. the behaviour that other people observe).

Throughout your life, many people have influenced your behaviour, in both positive and negative ways. When we are growing up, we unconsciously model our behaviour on that of our parents and other authoritative figures, and as we go on growing, we begin to model our behaviour on our peers. Sometimes we do this more consciously than others, but most of the time we are unaware of the influence other people have on how we behave.

There have been people in my life who have influenced me a great deal. Some of them in ways that I am not consciously aware of and others who have inspired me to consciously change my thinking and my behaviour. I have also on occasion sought to understand what psychology (internal activity) and physiology (external activity) drives the behaviour of people I admire and respect, with the conscious intent to adopt some of their behaviours to enhance my own effectiveness. Of course, I have only ever chosen to adopt behaviours that fit with my own vision or plan.

So, for instance, when I began looking at how I was going to market a new product through the internet, I chose to subscribe to lots of experts' email lists through signing up for their free eBooks or newsletters. As a result, I became a recipient of their marketing messages. Each of these 'experts' took a slightly different approach to their messaging in terms of their content and their process. Some were in my email inbox from the following day and every single day thereafter (until I unsubscribed!). Some were infrequent with their contact and so I slipped through their net. Some talked solely about their own products and services. Others shared the content of other people as well as their own content. Some sent long conversational emails, some told stories and others sent short, to the point messages. One marketer stood out for me. She was frequent enough in her contact for me to notice her, but not enough to irritate me. Her content was short and to the point, but equally it was engaging and of genuine value to me. She talked my language and she led me down a path where I bought from her. I went from being on her marketing list to being a paying customer and this impressed me.

So, when it came to deciding on my own marketing strategy, I started to pay even more attention to hers. I paid attention to her language, her education, her attitude and how she demonstrated those things through her messaging, and I sought to understand how what she was doing was engaging me. I made a note of my observations, and when it came to sitting down with my digital PA to discuss my own internet marketing strategy, I was able to reference her style and to build my own strategy based on that. This is just one example of where I have applied modelling to achieve an aspect of my vision.

Modelling is incredibly powerful. When you observe someone achieving the very thing you want to achieve, it makes sense to pay attention to how they are doing it and then, if what they are doing suits your own values, it makes sense to also adopt some of their behaviours.

Sometimes, that person is accessible to you and it is appropriate to ask them what they are doing. Other times, it isn't appropriate to do that, and it means observing them at a distance. Often people openly share what they do that makes them successful and how, through their education as part of their offering. I know, I do. In fact; I am doing it right now. You are working through the very process right now that I have used personally to attract success, and you are perhaps considering adopting some of my psychology and physiology to enhance yours.

ACTivity 6 in The ACT Of ACTION section on page 153 will guide you through modelling *attractive* behaviour.

YOUR PLAN

The word 'plan' means, 'a method of acting, doing, proceeding or making, developed in advance'. Planning in a business context refers to the process of setting goals and then developing the strategy (long-term action plan), including activities, with timescales, to achieve them.

It has been shown time and time again that people who set goals achieve more than those who don't. However, a plan is more than just goal setting. A plan is a documented account of the intended action to be taken and by when to achieve those goals. It details everything that needs to be done, when it is to be done, how it is to be done and by whom.

It still surprises me how few business people plan their business activity. And, I'm not talking about a traditional business plan either. A business plan is a financial document that provides evidence of a viable market and business opportunity, often for the purpose of raising capital – many business plans get written and then put in a drawer, never to be seen again. A plan of action is something quite different. A plan of action is a documented guide to achieving the business vision and so, by definition, it is a document that inspires and energises those in the business to take action.

Planning is so important in the creation of outcomes. I have seen so many business people fail to create the outcomes they intend because of failing to plan. I have also seen phenomenal success occur with relative ease due to simple planning. My greatest, fastest and most consistent business successes are as a result of a clearly defined vision and an appropriate plan of action.

To a great extent, if you've done 'the work' throughout this book, it has been in preparation for this part. You have documented your vision, decided on the qualities of your new mind-set and how you want to behave and be perceived by others. These elements are a powerful combination, but on their own, they will not result in the success you want. Now you need to put some structure around it all so they become the components of a plan that focuses your activity on that which will make your vision reality.

Whereas your vision provides the destination (your 'what') and the fuel (your 'why'), it's your plan of action that provides the directions (your 'how'). Your plan of action is your commitment to developing the beliefs, thoughts, feelings and behaviours to progress towards your vision day by day, and it encompasses the activities you need to do to ensure that your action is focused and that you take continual and daily conscious action to make it happen.

A word on Action: You'll have heard the advice: "do something, anything – just take action!" On one level, I agree: clearly doing nothing towards making your goals reality won't create results and so some activity is preferable to none at all. But, whilst doing 'anything' might result in *more* than doing nothing, that doesn't mean that *more* is always positive or productive.

Many people spend their time 'doing', but what they actually achieve is disproportionately less than the amount of energy they expend. Activity itself is not effective, and, poorly aligned activity can create more problems than not doing any at all. Trust me, I've seen it!

I've known people to take action continually and yet achieve very little. I have worked with people who believed that doing lots and lots of activity was an effective business strategy because 'some of that activity has to work' and as long as 50% of it did, that was a positive outcome. Hmm. The reality was that the hours spent (usually by other people) clearing up the impact of the 50% that didn't work often meant that the value of the activity that did work just wasn't worth it overall. Poorly aligned activity can be akin to wheel spinning – it depletes our resources, including our energy, and it gets us nowhere, and in extreme cases it sprays muck everywhere in the process, creating more work and less time and energy to do activity that would work!

So, sometimes, taking action is better than doing nothing, and sometimes the right thing to do is **nothing at all**, because when doing nothing at all is coming from a place of consciousness, then it's still 'doing'.

Success is reliant on taking positive action. Notice my intentional use of the word 'positive'. 'Positive' action is action that is affirmative – action that has intent. In other words, it's about activity which is aligned with your vision and that will positively impact your business and transform it into the business you want it to be. You need a *Plan* of Action!

As I said, your vision is the big picture – it's the destination, your plan is how you get there – it's the journey, and a journey by definition is an incremental experience. Sometimes, when people have a vision, they tend to aim for the 'big picture' outcome. The problem with that is that the outcome is so far in the future, it's hard to connect with it on a day-to-day basis, which makes it difficult to plan daily and weekly activities. It also makes it more difficult to see the light at the end of the tunnel on the days when you're feeling less motivated.

The key is to keep the destination (vision) in **view** but to keep the **focus** on the route and the road ahead. This means aiming for the next step in the plan and then the next, rather than the overall outcome. Not only does this mean that you are more likely to arrive at your destination, but it means that you expend less energy getting there, so you are more likely to enjoy the journey along the way.

Planning is one those things that we all know we should do, but that very few put the time in to do. Often that's because planning is seen as a time-consuming and complicated activity that restricts creativity and gets in the way of running the business. The reality is that good planning enables you to run your business **whilst** you also grow it. Growing your business without a plan is like getting in your car to drive to a destination to which you have never been without directions – you are likely to end up somewhere else! Planning does not restrict creativity or the ability to adapt, and in fact a good plan provides a framework that enables creativity and adaptability.

A good plan takes into account the vision, details the goals (with timescales) to be achieved to reach it and provides a process for reaching those goals. And a good plan is a **simple** one. Just like a vision that doesn't motivate you to take action, a plan that isn't simple to follow is of little value.

In order to take your vision and make it reality, you need to break it down first into goals and then into activities, and the logical way to do this is to start with the end in mind. Start with the vision and work backwards, working out the goals that need to be reached and then the activities that need to be done and in what logical sequence to achieve it. This enables an activity list to be created which serves as both a driver of your activity and also a checklist for the plan.

Of course, adjustments can be made in response to changing conditions, but that's the point, they are adjustments because the plan gives you something to work with.

Make sure your plan is *attractive*

Remember that this is The Act Of Attraction, so it's important to always keep *attraction* in mind when planning. No-one wants to feel like they are pushing, which is why an *attractive* plan is a gentle 'draw'.

Always consider: 'What activities are going to attract the right people and opportunities to me?' And then get that in your plan.

For example: if your vision talks about you speaking at large events, then you want to start by speaking at every opportunity. This means *attracting* the opportunity in the first place (which means also being open to receiving it) and then seizing it when it comes.

If your vision includes working with a particular type of client, then you might want to start to follow that type of client on social media and to ask people you know who they know who fits that profile. If your vision has a spacious living or working environment, then you might want to begin to create that in your current environment. I don't recommend knocking down walls, but you can get rid of clutter, sort out your filing and cupboards and create more space in your current environment.

Remember: like attracts like, so start taking the kind of action now that will attract the outcome you want.

If you have a full diary then you do not have the space for the new things to come in. This is not *attractive*. What **is** *attractive* is creating the space to allow the new things to occupy it.

For instance, this book was something I committed to when I already had a relatively full workload. In order to allow myself the time to write the book, I had to make it a priority in my mind and then actively create the space to do it. It meant removing some commitments from my diary and ceasing to do certain things during the three months I allocated to write the book. It also meant planning my book writing sessions as part of my overall action plan so that I stuck to them.

CREATING YOUR PLAN

An *attractive* plan is one based on: What > Why > When > Who > How

- o **What** is to be achieved? GOALS

- o **What** is to be done to achieve it? ACTIVITIES

- o **Why** is it to be achieved? PURPOSE

- o **When** is it to be done? TIMESCALES

- o **Who** is to do it? PEOPLE (skills and strengths)

- o **How** will it be done? METHOD

When your plan incorporates all of the above, you have every base covered. This enables you to (for the most part) simply follow the steps in your plan without having to concern yourself too much with what's up ahead, whilst also allowing you to adapt to changing conditions.

Setting goals

Whilst your goals relate to your vision, they are much more specific. Think of your vision as being the destination towards which you are moving and then think of your goals as being like landmarks along the way – they give you something to aim for.

So, if your vision includes a team, offices, a reputation as the best supplier of x services and 10 x your current revenue, then you may need to achieve things like: new website, new branding, new offices, admin person, etc. Within each goal, there will be activities that need to be done to achieve it, but at this stage, it's identifying the goals that's important.

For example, if part of the vision is you speaking in front of 1,000 people, then one goal might be to 'have a speaking engagement every month between now and x month'.

In the same way that your vision needs to motivate you to take action, so do your goals, so make them Positive, Purposeful, Precise, Parallel and Practical:

Positive means 'affirmative' so make sure your goals are based on your intent, and on what you want, as opposed to what you don't want. **Purposeful** means that they relate to your 'why'. **Precise** is about being specific. Vague goals are hard to achieve, as it's difficult to decide on the steps needed to achieve them. "I want to earn more money" is wishful thinking. "Increase monthly revenue by £15,000" is a goal. **Parallel** means that your goals are in line with each other. If you have conflicting goals, you may fail to achieve any of them. And, **Practical** is about ensuring that they are achievable. Whilst your vision is bold and stretches the current reality, your goals need to be challenging enough to motivate you, but also, they need to be perceived to be achievable.

So, in order to make your vision a reality, what goals do you need to achieve? Don't worry just yet about 'how'; just get clear on 'what'.

ACTivity 7 in The Act Of ACTION section on page 157 will guide you through setting your goals.

Defining activities

In the same way that your goals are defined by your vision, your activities are defined by your goals. Activities are the things that must be done – the steps that must be taken to reach the goals.

If your vision is your destination and provides the direction, and your goals are your landmarks, then your activities are the mileage you need to cover to get there.

So, what needs to be done in order to achieve the goals?

This is the process I use with my clients to turn their goals into a detailed plan of action.

1. List it

First we list everything that needs to happen to achieve each goal. Just like with goal setting, the 'how' is not a consideration at this stage. Some people find listing all the activities they need to do a bit daunting – as the list grows, the reality of what needs to be done can create anxiety. However, for some the act of writing it all down is very liberating as it gets it out of their head, freeing their mind up to focus on the next step of planning.

Whatever the case for you, trust me on this, downloading all of the things you need to get done is essential if you are to develop a plan of action that is both motivating and effective.

2. Order it

Doing things in the right order ensures that you don't get held up because something that should have been done earlier hasn't been done. So, next we list what needs to happen before what and then order the activities logically. So, for example, if the goal is to run an event and one activity is 'send out invitations', then the activities 'print invitations' and 'book venue' go before it.

3. Time it

Once we have a list of activities ordered in a logical sequence, we need to allocate timescales to them. We can't do this until we are clear on how long each activity will take and that means understanding what's involved.

4. Cost it

Whether it's the cost of your time, or the cost of materials or services, every activity has a cost associated with it. Cost can involve the use of any of the following resources: money, people, materials, services, transport, and in most instances this means a financial cost of some kind. We attribute the cost of materials and services to those activities and then consider the cost of any activities that require the time of the people in the business that will impact on the revenue.

5. Prioritise It

Once we have all activities in a logical sequence and understand how long each activity will take and what the resourcing requirements are, we prioritise them. Prioritising is different to ordering. A particular activity may fit in logically in one place but the costs associated may prevent it from being done at that time. This is why we cost everything first. Prioritising is about ensuring that the things that must be done first are done whilst not putting an unnecessary and risky strain on the financial resources of the business.

6. Delegate it

Even if you are a sole service provider business owner, you do not need to do all the activities yourself. Even if you are fully capable of doing them, it is highly likely that some activities would be best done by someone other than you. Sometimes, because we know we are capable of completing an activity ourselves, we think we should do it. Sometimes, we make that decision because we think it's the more cost-effective one and yet often the reality is that it takes us twice as long as someone else and effectively costs the business twice as much.

So, we look at the activities and identify **everything** that could be done by someone else. Then we go back over those activities and identify the ones that absolutely **must** be done by someone else (i.e. the activities that you absolutely **can't** do yourself). When we look at what's left, we can ask ourselves, what else **could** we delegate to free up the people in the business who can generate more revenue to pay for it?

A word on delegation. When you delegate something, you need to ensure that you give that person the authority they need to make it happen. You can only hold someone accountable if you give them both the responsibility and the authority to get the job done.

7. Document it

Just like your vision, your plan needs to be documented so that it exists in some form other than in your head. Documenting your plan involves more than just detailing the goals and activities required to make it reality – you also need to detail how you will ensure that you keep on track.

ACTivity 8 in The ACT Of ACTION section on page 159 will guide you through creating your plan.

KEEPING ON TRACK

Once you've got a vision and you know what you're doing and why, you're conditioned internally for success, and you have a plan of action, you're all sorted, right? Well, sort of.

Whilst in an ideal world a plan that is based on a vision that leverages intent and purpose should be enough to ensure activity, the reality is that often it isn't. I've yet to come across a vision and a plan of action that generates activity. Your vision might motivate it and your plan might direct it, but YOU have to actually DO it!

I know that's obvious and it might even sound a bit patronising, but if you've ever written a 'to do' list in the morning and not looked at it again until the evening only to find that nothing on it got done, you'll know exactly what I'm getting at!

Action means you actually 'doing' the things that are on the plan, and whilst that is obvious, it's not always what happens. That's why I always insist on implementing accountability measures into every plan of action.

Accountability Measures

So, what is an accountability measure?

Accountability is often described as 'being responsible for something'. Actually that's what responsibility means. Accountability is not just about being responsible for something – it is about being answerable for it too. Whilst for some, being responsible for an outcome is enough motivation to do it, for many, it just isn't. Many of us need to be held accountable too, and by that I mean, to know that someone else is aware of that responsibility and that their interest in the outcome will translate if necessary to actively ensuring that you do it.

I am a big believer in accountability. Perhaps because I have seen how a lack of it impacts negatively on results in previous roles and perhaps because, without it, I am 50% as effective as I am with it. I have achieved a lot in my life and have been involved in coaching and supporting others to achieve a lot in theirs too. What I have observed is that when someone has a vested interest in someone else's success to the extent that they will actively seek to see them achieve it, the other person tends to achieve more and faster. What I have observed in myself is that when I commit to someone else to deliver something by a certain time and particularly if that person is reliant on my delivering that in order for them to progress or succeed, I always deliver. Always.

As a result, I very consciously apply this pressure to myself in my business – in other words, I actively leverage the thing that I know makes me perform. This is an example of an accountability measure. Quite simply, an accountability measure is whatever it takes to make sure the job gets done!

I use this with my clients too. Once we get to the planning stage, I always ask the question: "What will make you do this?" I get varying responses and often we end up discussing first all the things that will make them **not** do it, before we are able to identify what will. Usually, the accountability measures we implement are based on either a 'towards', or an 'away from' motivation.

'Towards' and 'Away From' Motivation

As human beings, we are all conditioned to seek pleasure and avoid pain. However, the extent to which we are motivated more 'towards' and 'away from' is different depending on the person. People who are motivated 'towards' something are concerned with benefits – the outcome they'll get if they do it, whereas people who are motivated 'away from' something are more concerned with consequences – the outcome they'll get if they don't.

When I explain this to people, some assume that the right way to be is 'towards' motivated. The truth is that there is no ideal and in fact, even if there was, my view is this: so what? It's more difficult to change how we are motivated than it is to simply leverage whatever it is that motivates us in order to make us more effective.

I am personally more 'away from' motivated (you may have spotted that earlier). I am more concerned with the consequences of my not completing something than I am with the benefits of doing it, so rather than seek to change that in myself, I simply leverage it in my business. I purposely work with results-focused businesses that have drive and passion and high expectations of me, because I know that makes me deliver.

What about you? Are you 'towards' or 'away from' motivated? Are you more 'benefits' or more 'consequences' focused? It doesn't matter which is more you, what matters is that when you're implementing accountability measures, you leverage the one that is.

For many of my clients, the answer to the question "What will make you do this?" is having someone else drive their activity. Now, this may not seem like a very positive solution. You may feel that it's better to implement a more self-leadership type of accountability measure and you might be right. However, my view is this: if having someone else drive your plan means that you will do what you have committed yourself to doing for your own benefit, then implementing that measure is preferable to not.

I have performed this role for a number of my clients and also my friends. I have become their boss (at their invitation) and have been the person in their business to whom they are answerable. Every time it has worked and they have achieved what they set out to achieve.

Whatever will work – implement that as part of the plan. This way, you do not leave your results to chance.

Get a Coach or a Mentor

Every single one of my clients has recognised the value in having someone to support them in their business. The truth is, not one of us has the full tool kit required to develop and run a business. The attitude and the skills required to get a business off the ground are quite different to those required to manage a business that's already established. If we had all of the skills required to both start and run a business, we'd not excel at anything. Recognising this makes admitting to lacking skills in certain areas more appealing. Everyone needs support and guidance and some of us need directing to operate at our best. This is the value in hiring a coach or a mentor.

I say a coach OR a mentor because contrary to what many people think, although many coaches do an element of mentoring and many mentors also have coaching skills, the two roles are fundamentally very different.

Coaching is the process of enabling an individual to identify issues and solutions through skilled facilitation, whereas mentoring is the process of enabling an individual to achieve success through literally following in the path of someone who has done it.

A coach is typically someone that you hire to support you with a specific issue or project, and for a specified amount of time. Coaching itself is a set of skills that enable the coach to observe and analyse your attitude, skills and behaviour and to provide you with an objective perspective in order to enable you to develop and grow. A coach is focused specifically on your personal development and learning, and a business coach is focused on this with the specific aim of supporting you in your business.

Coaching involves questioning techniques to explore the individual's wants, needs, motivations, skills and thought processes so that they can identify their own solutions and set goals and activities to achieve them. It is not essential or even necessary for a business coach to have run a business, or to have any previous knowledge of the individual's area of expertise, industry, or product. Their value is defined by their ability to guide and support their client in identifying the areas for development and in identifying solutions.

A good coach is someone whom you respect and whom you feel respects you. A good coach is someone you feel comfortable talking openly and honestly with and by whom you are prepared to be challenged.

A mentor on the other hand is someone who has specific skills and experience in the area you want to develop those things. A business mentor is someone who has owned, developed and run a successful business and has demonstrated that they have the skills required to succeed. Anyone in this position will have had failings a well as successes and it is their ability to turn a failing into a success that makes their input into your business so valuable.

Ideally they have had experience running businesses similar to yours; however, the industry is less important than the type of business it is. For instance, if you sell services, a good mentor for you is someone who has built and run a business that sells services.

A mentor may be someone you pay to support you, or it may be a friend or a previous boss or colleague who shares their experience and wisdom willingly. A good mentor is someone who has an investment in your success. They help you to explore options and solutions and to understand and deal with obstacles so that you can make informed decisions. For this reason, a good mentor will always be honest with you. They will tell you if they think an idea you have is too risky and they will tell you if they don't know something, and ideally, they will also have an extensive network of other experts and suppliers to leverage to get the right answer. They take your best interests to heart and they are committed to helping you achieve your business goals. A mentor is the person to whom you turn for advice and direction and is the first to hear of your successes.

I have a great mentor with whom I discuss all aspects of my business and I hire a coach when I need one. In fact, I hired a coach to support me through the process of writing this book and that investment ensured that I completed the entire process in just 90 days.

Both a coach and a mentor play an important role in your success. However, neither one of them is responsible for it. Remember self-leadership? It's your life. It's your business. It's your vision. It's your plan. You are ultimately responsible.

Share your plan

Do you remember my advice about sharing your vision? I suggested it because sharing it creates the accountability you need to follow-through. It is unlikely that you are the only person who this plan affects, so rather than just sharing the specific activity that affects the person whose responsibility it is to do it, share the entire plan (or at least the bit that relates to that specific goal) with everyone who either contributes to it, or is affected by it. By engaging them in your plan, you make it more real for them and for you, and because it becomes 'collaborative', you all commit to it on a wholly different level.

Use 'qualifiers'

Sometimes new opportunities present themselves, which are not part of our vision or plan. Whilst it's important to remain open to new opportunities, it can also be easy to allow them to distract us and take us off track. Having some qualifiers (pre-determined questions) that you ask yourself whenever you are presented with something new makes it easier to make the decision about whether or not to go with it. I used this myself when I was building my first business. My vision was driven by two fundamental values: to work with people I liked and to do what I was passionate about. Sometimes an opportunity would present itself which on the surface appeared to be in line with the intent aspect of my vision (the things I wanted to achieve), but when I asked myself the questions: "Do I like them?" or "Am I passionate about it", the answer was no. So, I didn't do it. Simple.

What qualifiers could you create that reflect your intent and purpose as part of your plan to keep you on track? The question needs to be answered with a 'yes' in order for you to consider it. If the answer is 'no', or 'maybe', you simply discard it.

Celebrate your wins

I am a big believer in celebrating wins. We are often our greatest critic, and find it easier to notice the things we've not achieved, or that haven't changed, than we are at noticing the things that have.

I have a fabulous client, a newly qualified physiotherapist who started his practice with no money, no premises and no clients. Together we created a vision that leveraged his intent and purpose and a three-month plan of action. The plan included a brand, logo, website, marketing strategy (with financial projections). In three months, he surpassed his financial projections and was able to cover his business and personal outgoings. To me that's an incredible win! Newly qualified and already turning over enough to cover all expenses. What a great position to build from.

For him, it was a good outcome, but he was concerned that the two months coming up looked quiet – it was true, they did. Clearly, having achieved and surpassed the goals in the previous plan, we needed to create another plan to take his business to the next level, and of course, that's what we did. But, I insisted that before we do that, we discussed and documented what he'd achieved to date and that he celebrated it.

There are two reasons for this: 1) just because, actually, it feels good and it's good for our self-esteem to notice and celebrate the things we do well, and 2) because like attracts like which means that success attracts more of it. Celebrating is *attractive.*

So, make an effort to acknowledge each step you take along your plan and towards your vision and then celebrate those small wins. This doesn't have to mean anything big. It could be dinner out, or a massage or film, but it could just be a glass of wine, or as simple as telling someone about it. How you mark it is not important. What is important is that you acknowledge it because the more you bring your success into conscious awareness, the more you will be motivated to achieve more of it. Like attracts like.

Dealing with time

For some, once they get to the planning stage and look at their diary, they find it a sobering moment as they realise that it is chock-a-block and they have no space at first glance to do very much at all towards their plan. If this is you, then you're not alone. It's often the case that prior to planning, time is not being used efficiently. However, you know that if you want to make your business the success that you have defined, you need to give the steps required to achieving it high priority.

Remember that whatever is in your diary got there because you said yes to it. So, identify anything in your schedule that could be either removed or moved. Then make an effort to cluster activities of a similar nature together (like client work), and move non work-related activities to outside of your working day. If this feels a bit uncomfortable, be clear: it's not forever. It's for the period you are focusing on this priority.

Clear your desk of anything that is not completed, either by completing it, or by deciding it's not important – you'd be surprised how distracting uncompleted activities can be on a subconscious level.

Let people know how much time you can give them and stick to it and only ever spend as much time on an activity as it deserves.

Dealing with procrastination

Procrastination is the act of putting off essential activities. Sometimes it manifests in doing non-essential activities instead and sometimes it manifests in doing none at all. Procrastination is something we have all experienced.

It's normal to experience an emotional reaction when we have to do something that we don't want to do, or that we are convinced we can't do. However, when this happens consistently to the extent that it results in no activity at all, then it is a problem. It gets in the way of our progress and it also affects our self-esteem, which is incredibly *unattractive*.

Completion of activities creates a sense of satisfaction and increases self-esteem. No matter how small, the act of completing something creates the very thing you need to complete more things. So, if you find that despite all your planning, you are rooted in 'in-action', here are some simple strategies to help get you moving:

Start with the easy stuff. Ask yourself "What simple thing can I do today that will definitely move me **forward** in my plan and **towards** my goal?" And then do that first. Everyone can answer this question. The challenge is never in identifying the next step; the challenge is in doing it. It might be as simple as making a phone call, or even just obtaining the phone number. It might be adding some copy to your website, or changing it. It might be commenting on someone's blog or watching a webinar. In fact, make step one easy intentionally and then, whatever it is, do that first!

The psychology behind this is to get activity happening – to get things moving. Remember, like attracts like and so one activity will generate more activity. You just need to get started.

So, back to the advice earlier: 'do something, do anything'. Do anything **as long as it will result in an outcome that moves you forward in your plan and closer to your vision**. Forward movement is positive and it's a lot easier to move forward when you're already moving.

And, if you're really not feeling it, then take the time out. Don't push water uphill – that's not *attractive* either!

If you find that you are procrastinating on a daily basis, then I would suggest that there is a weakness in your vision and most likely with the *purpose* aspect – your 'why' is not compelling enough and it's probably time to revisit it.

The ACT Of ACTION
(ACTivities)

Go to www.theactofattraction.com to
download these worksheets

YOUR BEHAVIOUR

ACTIVITY 5:
IDENTIFY YOUR REPUTATION

Identify your current reputation so that you can ensure that in future it supports your vision.

Remember, reputation is the estimation or opinion in which you are commonly held by others. Whilst you are who you are based on your values, beliefs and behaviours, your reputation is driven by other people's **perception** of who you are and is the by-product of what they think and say about you.

An *attractive* reputation is one that supports your vision (it is intentional and purposeful), which shows in the behaviour that other people observe. An *attractive* reputation is one that attracts desired people, circumstances and opportunities to you. An *attractive* reputation is one that is consistent regardless of the social group (work, social, family, etc) and which is formed through repeated, consistent behaviour over time.

WORKSHEET 5   YOUR BEHAVIOUR – REPUTATION

Think for a minute about who you are and what you stand for. List those things here.

Now think about how your behaviour represents those things: in your business, in your network and in your social interactions. Does your behaviour back up who you present yourself to be? And, more importantly, are you comfortable that other people's perception of you is in line with that?

Then answer the following questions:

What do you think other people think of you?

What things do you know other people say about you?

What things have been written about you, or relayed back to you?

What do you know you are you known for?

How would you describe your reputation?

If you find this activity easy, then the chances are you have a good grasp on your reputation. If you don't, then it's probably time to start paying more attention.

YOUR BEHAVIOUR

ACTIVITY 6: MODEL BEHAVIOUR

Model behaviour that is aligned with your vision to enhance your own success

Remember, modelling is the process of recreating excellence through studying any human behaviour and mastering the psychology (beliefs and thoughts) and physiology (reactions and actions) that underlie that behaviour. It is the process of achieving an outcome by studying how someone else has gone about achieving the same outcome and then applying the same behaviour.

Modelling is incredibly powerful. When you observe someone achieving the very thing you want to achieve, it makes sense to pay attention to how they are doing it, and then if what they are doing suits your own values, it makes sense to also adopt some of their behaviours.

WORKSHEET 6   YOUR BEHAVIOUR – MODEL BEHAVIOUR

Throughout this book, you have highlighted the thoughts, feelings and behaviours you want to possess and exhibit and how you want them to manifest in your reputation in order to achieve your vision.

Think about these things now and consider the people around you who you know (either personally or through other means) who already exhibit the behaviours and/or skills that you want to adopt?

Who springs to mind?

What specifically do they do?

How do they do it?

<u>What behaviour traits do they have that you aspire to have?</u>

(It may be that they talk about a way that they prepare themselves for success, or how they deal with challenges and hurdles. Perhaps it's the way they promote or market themselves. Perhaps it's their style of writing that appeals to you.)

This is easy for some people and others find it difficult. The following questions may help:

<u>Who do I aspire to be more like?</u>

It may be helpful to think of someone who exhibits the exact opposite of what you aspire to be and then think of someone who does the opposite to them.

The qualities I need to develop

If you still find this challenging, try this:

Imagine that someone has given you a magic pill that will give you the aspects of that person's behaviour that you desire. Within 10 minutes of taking this pill, you can feel yourself changing. What changes take place?

YOUR PLAN

ACTIVITY 7:
SET YOUR GOALS

Turn your vision into goals so that you have a structure for your activity

Remember, a plan is a documented account of the intended action to be taken and by when to achieve those goals. It details everything that needs to be done, when it is to be done, how it is to be done and by whom.

Whilst your goals relate to your vision, they are much more specific. Think of your vision as being the destination towards which you are moving and then think of your goals as being like landmarks along the way – they give you something to aim for.

In the same way that your vision needs to motivate you to take action, so do your goals, so remember to make them Positive, Purposeful, Precise, Parallel and Practical.

So, in order to make your vision a reality, what goals do you need to achieve?

WORKSHEET 7   YOUR PLAN – GOAL SETTING

Have a look at your vision. What goals do you need to achieve in order to make it reality? Don't worry just yet about 'how' you are going to do it, just get clear on 'what' needs to be achieved and write it down

YOUR PLAN

ACTIVITY 8:
DEFINE YOUR ACTIVITIES

Turn your goals into a plan of action so that your activity is focused and moves you towards your vision

Remember, in the same way that your goals are defined by your vision, your activities are defined by your goals. Activities are the things that must be done – the steps that must be taken to reach the goals.

If your vision is your destination and provides the direction, and your goals are your landmarks, then your activities are the mileage you need to cover to get there.

So, what activities need to be done in order to achieve the goals?

WORSHEET 8   YOUR PLAN – DEFINE ACTIVITIES

The easiest way to plan activities is to create a spreadsheet. This will enable you to move things around and to change things as you progress through the plan with ease.

Create a spreadsheet with the following columns:

GOAL	ACTIVITY	TIME	COST	WHO

1. List it

List everything that needs to happen to achieve the goal. Include all the steps you need to take including anything that came out of the activities in this book. For instance, if you need to go back and do the activities, include that in the list. If you identified something you need to do as a result of doing an activity, then list that too.

Just like when you were setting the goals, do not concern yourself right now with 'how' or 'when' you will do these things, just list them all.

2. Order it

Doing things in the right order ensures that you don't get held up because something that should have been done earlier hasn't been done. Ask yourself, what needs to happen before what and then order the activities logically.

3. Time it

Now that you have a list of activities ordered in a logical sequence, you want to start to allocate timescales to them. However, you can't do this until you are clear on how long each activity will take. So, consider how long each activity will take (be realistic!) and put the amount of time to be allocated into the TIME column of your spreadsheet.

4. Cost it

Whether it's the cost of your time, or the cost of materials or services, every activity you do has a cost associated with it. Remember, cost can involve the use of any of the following resources: money, people, materials, services, transport. Enter all costs into the spreadsheet in the COST column.

5. Prioritise It

Prioritising is different to ordering. A particular activity may fit into the plan somewhere logically but the costs associated may prevent it from being done at that time. This is why you have costed everything. Move any activity that needs to move down the list.

6. Delegate it

Look at the activities and identify everything that could be done by someone else and put their name or supplier type in the WHO column. Then go back over those activities and identify the ones that absolutely must be done by someone else (i.e. the activities that you absolutely can't do yourself). Now, look at what's left. What else could you still delegate to free you up to work on the things that will generate more revenue to pay for it?

7. Document it

Just like your vision, your plan needs to be documented so that it exists in some form, other than in your head. To a great extent, your plan is already documented in the spreadsheet you're completing, but documenting your plan involves more than just detailing the goals, time commitment and activities required to make it reality. You now need to allocate the days and weeks to those activities. You also need to detail how you will ensure that you keep on track.

Keeping on Track

What accountability measures will you implement?

What qualifiers will you use?

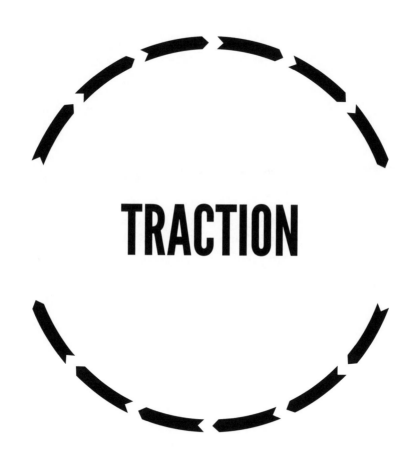

TRACTION

The Act Of Attraction is a process.

It begins with getting what's going on in your head right: your vision (so that you have a destination in mind), and your beliefs, thoughts and feelings, so that you are conditioned internally to achieve it. It's followed by getting what you're actually doing aligned with that vision, so that your behaviour and the impact on other people's perception attracts to you the people and opportunities you want, and the activities you undertake move you forward with intention and purpose.

When you have vision, beliefs, thoughts and feelings, behaviour and activity all aligned, that's when you gain Traction.

Traction is the cumulative effect of ATTRACT and ACTION. It's the feeling we get when what we have been focusing our efforts on starts to 'grip' and we begin to feel like we are progressing forwards effortlessly. All of our actions start to impact in all areas and we begin to experience a gentle 'draw' as opposed to the forced 'push' that is so often associated with effort. And, just like the state of Traction itself, the process of getting there creates momentum, propelling us forward to the next step.

When you have all the elements of The Act Of Attraction working together, your internal and external activity work in tandem and you begin to move forward with relative ease. That's because there is no tension between what's going on in your head and what's happening in reality. Your activity creates more activity so that you gain ground and results happen – so you cannot help but move forwards. This is how you begin to realise your vision!

By following The Act Of Attraction's 4-step process to creating business success, you begin to create the business you really **want**. And so, instead of looking back in three, six, twelve months' time and asking yourself why you've not moved forwards in your business, you can look back and ask yourself instead: "Where can I take my business next?"

WHAT NOW?

So, you've read the book. What are you going to do now?

Are you going to carry on as before and risk finding yourself where you are now in twelve months' time, or somewhere you didn't intend to be? Or, are you going to risk taking responsibility and accountability and consciously creating the conditions to attract the business of your dreams?

It's a serious question.

What would you **like** to be doing in a few years' time? What do you **want** people to be saying about you? What 'stories' would you **like** to share with your network, or your clients, or even your grandchildren? What would you like to be celebrating? What do you **want**?

It's your life so you decide on the destination. It's your life so you decide on the journey. It's your life, so you decide on the people you take along for the ride.

So, when would **now** be the right time to get in the driver's seat?

To your success!

If you enjoyed the book, why not visit
www.theactofattraction.com
for free downloads and resources.

MY STORY

My early career took an operational management route within the oil and gas industry, before I moved into human resources management within investment banking.

We'd not had much money as I was growing up and lacked many things that these days most of us take for granted. Life was a struggle and I can recall both the practical and emotional impact on the family of significant money worries. However, there was an underlying message when I was growing up that there would 'always be enough'. And there was.

I was relatively academic and I did well at school and although I went to college to do my A Levels, the truth is, I couldn't wait to get out to work. That motivation was driven by a desire to get earning and to be 'successful' (quote, unquote).

Armed with a vision of what this 'successful' life looked like (own property, nice car, good job and relationship, etc), I did what came naturally – I planned it.

From the age of 18, I climbed the corporate ladder, starting in a data entry role within the telecoms industry, and moving into sales support within the oil and gas industry. I very quickly developed a passion for the 'people' element of business and so while my career took a line-management route, I went back to college part-time to study HR. I bought my first car at 18, my first flat at 22, in Chelsea in London, I achieved every promotion I applied for and climbed the corporate ladder with ease. The planning worked.

A few years later, I was promoted into a job I had wanted for two years, managing a team of account managers. After six months, when my colleague in a neighbouring department went on maternity leave, I was 'asked' to take on responsibility for her team as well as my own. At 26 years old, I had two jobs, 22 staff and with limited support from the senior management team, I burned out.

I remember the day my back seized up like it was yesterday. I was bending over to plug the vacuum cleaner into the socket and I heard it click. I was stuck rigid. Unable to straighten up, let alone walk, I crawled to the phone and in agony I told my mum what had happened. Her response? "Are you listening yet?"

Over two bed-ridden weeks (and after a fair amount of 'listening' (!)), it dawned on me that whilst I'd ticked most of my 'success' boxes; somewhere along the line I'd got it spectacularly wrong.

A friend recommended a Hypnotherapist in London and over four months I saw her every week. Within a couple of sessions, I had learned to manage my stress and I could have stopped there, but the experience of working with the mind, opened my eyes to a whole new realisation: that we have control over our lives through the way we choose to think and feel and, in effect, how we behave. Those sessions changed my life.

I made the decision then to create the life I really wanted and to follow my passion: the development of people. Naturally, I aimed high and applied for an HR manager role at a large investment bank. I had nine interviews for the job (yes nine!), before being offered the job of my dreams. I remember holidaying in Sydney and them having to fax the contract to me in my hotel room so that I could start on the first working day of the year 2001.

I recall how impressed I was with the employee benefits – no-one had human resources sewn up like these guys: there were on-site doctors and dentists, and an on-site restaurant. There was even an on-site crèche, so, if the child-minder was sick, you could bring the kids to work! There was a concierge service which meant that if your washing machine was sick, you could simply make a call and the concierge team would organise a plumber for you, come to your desk, collect your keys, go to your house, let the plumber in, supervise the work and return your keys to you before you left the office. It was textbook perfect and I remember feeling that I'd really landed on my feet.

It was about two weeks in when I realised that whilst on the surface this all appeared to be supporting the wellness of the staff, the reality on the ground was that no-one had any excuse not to be at their desk. Ever.

I remember the realisation that I'd done it again. In pursuit of 'success', I'd pursued a conventional route without stopping to define what I really wanted, or what was really important to me. In fact, by convincing nine individual people that I was not only the right person for the job, but the right culture fit for the organisation, I'd massively compromised my personal values. Once again, I'd achieve what was on my plan, but what I'd effectively done was planned myself into being miserable. I began to feel resentful at the organisation and angry with myself. I felt like a fraud.

With my city job, my great salary and lifestyle and my nice car and flat, I appeared 'successful'. Everyone around me considered me to be, and yet, I didn't feel it at all. In fact, I was deeply unhappy and I felt like a failure.

I had two significant realisations then: 1. That I had walked myself down this path and that I had no-one to blame but myself, and 2. That I was incredibly capable of creating outcomes and if I put half as much effort into setting the right goals as I did into planning, I could create genuine success.

So, I got right back to basics. I began to focus my attention on the things that were really important to me (the things that made me 'feel' successful), like working with people I liked and doing things I was passionate about. Life suddenly got a lot simpler.

At 29, when all my friends were settling down and thinking about getting married and having children I abandoned the plan in quite a dramatic fashion and literally threw my life up in the air. I left the UK and over four years in Melbourne, Australia, I travelled and bummed around on beaches whilst working various jobs and studying psychology, psychotherapy and clinical hypnosis. Learning how to more effectively use my mind and how to teach others to do the same changed my entire outlook on life.

When I returned to the UK in 2006, it was a natural next step to set up my private practice.

I moved to a small town in South Wales and set up Alpha Therapy. With all my work experience being in sales support, operations and management, I had never built a business from scratch and I knew very little about marketing. All of my friends were in other parts of the country and none of them were in business for themselves, so I had no choice but to get out and meet people. So I went out networking.

I joined a small aspiring business-networking group in Cardiff, and seeing an opportunity to develop my own business through building a network, I offered to get involved with building the group. I became the group leader initially and a few months later I took on responsibility for developing a network of business breakfast groups in and around South Wales. Over 12 months, I developed a team and the business processes and training to establish 16 groups in the region, and in the process I developed a support structure for my own business. I developed my knowledge of sales and marketing and created a full and lucrative private practice.

During that time, I met the Director of Strategy, Tim Johnson, and was inspired by his vision and strategic plan to create a national business network where small businesses could support each other and develop the skills, confidence and competence to enable them to grow, both personally and professionally. I knew then I could add significant value to this vision and when he asked me to join the board of directors, my simple qualifiers "Do I like them?" and "Am I passionate about it?" made saying 'yes' an easy decision.

As a team of four directors, we built a national business network in four years. As the Network Director, it was my role to develop the network and so I applied the principles of vision, mind-set, behaviour (culture) and planning to develop the leadership, processes, systems and training to create a national team with a shared vision to develop a national business network across the country.

I now run my own business Alpha Associates Ltd (www.alpha-associates.biz), working with businesses who are serious about creating success to enable them to achieve their vision.

ABOUT THE AUTHOR

Ditching a successful HR and management career in the oil and gas and investment banking industries in 2002, Tamsen Garrie moved to Melbourne, Australia where over four years, she re-trained in psychology, clinical hypnotherapy and conflict resolution.

Moving back to the UK in 2006, Tamsen embarked on the journey of self-employment, setting up her own business in South Wales. She joined a small aspiring business network in the South West of England, and over 12 months developed the network in South Wales from one business networking group to a region of 16 groups whilst using that platform to build a successful clinical practice, enabling people to create significant success in their lives and businesses.

Tamsen joined the board of that business network as the Network Director in August 2008, and it was the powerful combination of corporate HR and operational management, strong leadership and an inherent understanding of people that enabled her to develop the infrastructure, including the leadership team, processes and training to enable its growth from that small local business network into the national business that it is today.

She now owns and runs Alpha Associates Ltd, a 'people and business development' company based in the South West of England. Her experience working with hundreds of businesses, training numerous leaders and developing numerous teams has resulted in a thorough understanding of the many challenges that are familiar to business owners. This coupled with her engaging communication style and her ability to work with all types of people makes her uniquely placed to work with businesses to develop the vision, mind-set, behaviour and plan to create significant business success.